Not since Rebecca Pippert's *Out of the Saltshaker and Into the World* twenty years ago have I come across a book that encouraged and motivated me evangelistically like *Never Ashamed*. With riveting stories from decades of witnessing to Jewish people, Avi Snyder melts away the fears that keep us silent when love demands we speak. Fun, practical, and timely.

—*Jim Congdon*
Senior pastor, Topeka Bible Church

Never Ashamed is a fresh, winsome retelling of the biblical narrative on evangelism. Through vivid analogy and personal story, Avi has crafted a compelling and inspiring case for personal witness. Reader beware, however: *Never Ashamed* is a deceptively simple, short book that will sneak up on the Christian spirit, reigniting a love for the lost and a passion for soul winning.

—*R. York Moore*
Executive director, Catalytic Partnerships
National evangelist and author

Avi Snyder peppers his teaching with parables/stories. Just like Jesus. He powerfully reminds us that the gospel is not simply "good" news; it is compelling, interesting, and, to use Avi's new term, "provocative." *Never Ashamed* is an overwhelming call to speak about Jesus, to tell the world that Jesus is believable and beautiful, to understand that we can trust the power of the seed. I have never felt more compelled and excited to share the gospel.

—*Michael Card*
Author and composer

I have known Avi for almost twenty years. He reminds me of the apostle Paul. He lives what he is writing about. And he did this for over thirty years in different contexts and cultures. That is one of the reasons why he is such a wonderful storyteller. His stories are powerful illustrations of this much-needed message to us Christians, pastors, and churches, which can help us to overcome timidity, fears, and excuses when it comes to sharing the gospel. Avi does not write about methods of evangelism, but why sharing the gospel is such a divine necessity, and why the presentation of the gospel should be clear and provoke a response. Avi is aware of the timidity and fears of the human heart and knows the excuses and reasons that shut our mouths. Therefore, he describes the various fruits and joys of sharing the gospel, and why he and the early Christians felt compelled to do so. The book is convincing. Reading Avi's book made me pray again: "Lord, fill my heart with your compassion for the lost."

—Dr. Dietrich Kuhl
Former international director, WEC International
(Worldwide Evangelism for Christ)

Something I have observed in many of my friends who are Jewish believers is they are the most courageous, outrageous, and passionate evangelists. Avi Snyder is one of these. I read *Never Ashamed* and couldn't put it down. It makes compelling reading. It challenges the notion that social action is enough. It is not. Proclamation is what's needed.

As Avi says, "The gospel must be communicated in love and with compassion. Why? Because the message itself is so cutting that it hardly needs any additional sharpening from us. The very first time that the Spirit filled the disciples, He filled them for no other reason than to empower them to proclaim. In other words, gospel proclamation was the very first manifestation of the Spirit's filling. The gospel is not just good news. The gospel is urgent news."

If you are a reluctant evangelist, reading this book will inspire and encourage you to proclaim the gospel effectively and with a fresh sense of urgency.

—*Julia Fisher*
Writer, broadcaster, director
The Olive Tree Reconciliation Fund

Never Ashamed comes out of Avi Snyder's international walk with Yeshua, and his passion to explain simply but powerfully how Messianic Jews and non-Jewish Christians should be bold in sharing their faith in Yeshua. Filled with great stories, good humor, surprising ideas, and thought-provoking perspectives, *Never Ashamed* will provoke both laughter and reflection while inspiring readers to renew their commitment to bringing Yeshua's salvation to Jews and non-Jews alike.

—*Dr. Byron Spradlin*
President, Artists in Christian Testimony International

Spread the word about Jesus! That is a life motto of Avi Snyder, who, with this book, continues and deepens his thoughts from *Jews Don't Need Jesus—and Other Misconceptions.* When reading the pages of this new book, *Never Ashamed: Stories of Sharing Faith with Scoffers and Skeptics,* we hear above all else the voice of a heart that has experienced the love of God and cannot remain silent about it. Avi draws on the wealth of experience from decades of personal evangelization in several continents and cultures. All of this is served with that special pinch of Jewish humor with which the author spices his statements and brings weighty truths to his readers. What would he want from his readers and the history of the impact of his book? Perhaps that we say after reading, "We cannot keep silent about what we have seen and heard ourselves!"

—*Klaus-Dieter Passon*
Editor-in-chief, *Charisma Magazine,* Germany

The gospel seems to be losing its weight in today's society. The postmodern or post-Christian world is not interested in being saved. But we Christians have a Jesus-given command to go and preach the gospel, and to make disciples of those who make a commitment to follow Jesus. Avi Snyder's book reminds us of this mandate. The command is still active, not completed, not taken back. Read this book, feel Avi's heart for sharing the gospel, and, as you go, be open to share the life-saving, life-changing message of the gospel! This book has challenged me, and I hope it will challenge you as well to share your faith—a faith that saves.

—*Attila Kapocs*
Regional director, Operation Mobilisation, Central Europe

It gave me great pleasure to read the manuscript of Avi Snyder's book *Never Ashamed: Stories of Sharing Faith with Scoffers and Skeptics.* I have known and held the author in respect for a number of years, becoming acquainted with him during his years of ministry in Hungary. His book commends itself for a number of reasons. It contains a clear challenge for both Jewish and non-Jewish readers to be unashamedly outspoken about their faith in Jesus Christ and the need for everyone to repent and turn to Jesus for forgiveness of their sins and a new life. This call is much needed in our day and age, when efforts are being made more than ever to marginalize the Christian faith, to push Jesus Christ out of the public discussion, and to cancel or persecute people who speak out about Him. The gospel message is the only solution to mankind's most fundamental problem, and Avi makes a strong case in his book for it being presented to all and sundry in compassionate and clearly understandable terms. This is the duty of every follower of the Messiah Jesus, Jewish and Gentile alike. In underpinning his arguments, Avi uses a plethora of quotes from both the Old and New Testaments of the Bible. His book is very readable; the different points the author makes are liberally illustrated by real-life examples taken from Avi's own life and ministry as well as other sources. I am persuaded that readers of this book will be spiritually uplifted and derive from it a renewed impetus to go and share the gospel with friends, relatives, colleagues, and all.

—Dr. Ákos Bukovszky
Head of the External Affairs Department,
Baptist Union of Hungary

Whenever I encounter Avi, God stirs my heart with a renewed passion to share the good news about Jesus, or Yeshua. *Never Ashamed* has revitalized my courage and confidence to share Jesus. I especially enjoyed the chapter on the fruits that God produces when we share the gospel as it reminded me of God's sovereignty through the gospel message. Each chapter uses biblical truth and winsome stories to build us up in our faith and our common responsibility to share Jesus with others. In a time when Christians tend to overcomplicate life in and through Jesus, Avi reminds us of the simple and straightforward truth of the Gospels. I will encourage every member of my church to read this book—and I look forward to the fruit it will bear for God's kingdom.

—Rev. Dr. Rodney Woods
City Temple, London

With wit, humor, and not a little passion, Avi Snyder distills the wisdom and experience of many years in this marvelous book. Avi's ministry in the USA, Russia, and Germany will inform and challenge you as he shares his encounters and recollections. A great storyteller, Avi knows how to communicate. With honesty, humility, and empathy, he details the challenges and opportunities he has been given in following the call of his Messiah Jesus to share the good news with Israel and all nations. As a preacher, he brings Scripture alive, illustrating it with personal insights and the principles that have shaped his discipleship and witness. Read and enjoy!

—Dr. Richard Harvey
Former academic dean, All Nations Christian College

I love to read. But I especially love to discover books that grip my soul and require me to pull out my yellow highlighter! It came out early into Avi Snyder's book. As I read his compelling stories, his powerful biblical application, and his encouraging challenges, my heart was stirred. I experienced those "aha!" moments that excite me when I read a book that requires response from me. In one story, Avi is referred to as a "provocateur." I agree. He is. So is his book. And I am so thankful God provoked me through *Never Ashamed: Stories of Sharing Faith with Scoffers and Skeptics.*

—*Lettie K. Whisman*
Author, *God's Extravagant Grace for Extraordinary Grief*

"Faithful are the wounds of a friend" echoed in my mind as I read *Never Ashamed*. With the *chutzpah* of a veteran street evangelist, Avi Snyder walks up to those of us who are lost when it comes to sharing the gospel and says, "I have good news you desperately need to hear." Through humor and storytelling, Snyder brings us to God's Word to show us the reasons why we struggle and why that struggle is worth overcoming. In a day when so many voices in the church call us to self-care, *Never Ashamed* calls us back to God's heart—care for the lost. Avi Snyder is the friend we all need.

—*Dan Strull*
Congregation leader, Olive Tree Messianic Congregation, Chicago, IL

AVI SNYDER

NEVER ASHAMED

STORIES OF SHARING FAITH WITH SCOFFERS AND SKEPTICS

W

WHITAKER
HOUSE

NEVER ASHAMED
Stories of Sharing Faith with Scoffers and Skeptics

avi.snyder@jewsforjesus.org

ISBN: 978-1-64123-873-1
eBook ISBN: 978-1-64123-874-8

Printed in the United States of America
© 2022 by Avi Snyder

Whitaker House
1030 Hunt Valley Circle
New Kensington, PA 15068
www.whitakerhouse.com

Library of Congress Cataloging-in-Publication Data (Pending)

1 2 3 4 5 6 7 8 9 10 11 ⨆⨆ 29 28 27 26 25 24 23 22

DEDICATION

Dedicated to Ruth

*The eternal God is your dwelling place, and underneath
are the everlasting arms.*
—Deuteronomy 33:27 ESV

Jesus said to them, "Come and have breakfast."
—John 21:12

CONTENTS

FOREWORD

I will never forget the time I was preaching on a Sunday morning at one of the larger megachurches in North America. The pastor concluded his introduction of me by asking the congregation of over ten thousand people to "please welcome a man who may just be the greatest Jewish evangelist since the apostle Paul!" As I stumbled my way up the steps to the podium, I was embarrassed, chagrined, and thinking to myself, *David, with an introduction like that, you can only go downhill from here.*

While I am quite sure I should never be introduced in such a fashion, I am not sure that Avi Snyder isn't deserving of such accolades. He is, for me, an example of a true evangelist in the mold of the apostle Paul. In fact, as a world-class dramatist, Avi even created a one-man play on the life of the apostle; if you saw it, it would have you believing, as I do, that this man carries in his heart and soul the passion of the greatest evangelist of all time.

Avi would not have it said that way about himself. His passion is kept in check by a deep humility, but he has never been retiring about his love for God and His gospel. Avi's latest book, *Never Ashamed*, perfectly captures that love for God and passion for the gospel. It is a lofty yet down to earth, soul-gripping invitation to consider afresh the greatest God-given task in history. Avi presents each chapter with delightful self-deprecating humor that good-naturedly flows from rich experience.

Avi doesn't just talk about evangelism. He is a consummate practitioner of evangelism. He practices it everywhere he goes. And Avi has gone just about everywhere in the world in his career of service with Jews for Jesus. He is the founder of our most fruitful ministry in the former Soviet Union as well as in Germany and Hungary. Along the way, he has had enough evangelistic experiences and opportunities to fill multiple books. Since Avi is a consummate storyteller, each and every point he makes in every chapter is wonderfully illustrated with a poignancy that will capture your heart.

Read this book to be inspired. Read this book to be instructed. Read this book to be motivated to join with Avi *and* with the apostle Paul in fulfilling that wonderful Great Commission. This is a calling God has given, not only to the expert evangelists like Avi Snyder, but to each one of us who would follow the Lord Jesus.

—David Brickner
Executive director, Jews for Jesus

INTRODUCTION:
THE GOSPEL AND GREEN PAINT

A number of years ago, a synagogue in Southern California hosted a panel discussion on the topic "Jews by Choice," and the organizers invited me to take part. I jumped at the invitation because it gave me the opportunity to present the gospel and to state what I've known ever since I became a follower of Yeshua—that since Jesus is the Messiah according to Moses and the prophets, then the most "Jewish choice" we can make is to believe in Him.

During the question-and-answer session that followed, a middle-aged man suddenly shot to his feet. "So, you want to believe what the gentiles believe and still call yourself a Jew?" he asked with unmasked contempt. "Fine. But why do you have to go around broadcasting your views to everybody else? Why can't you just keep your opinion to yourself and respect other people's points of view?"

> **I WAS ASKED, "WHY CAN'T YOU JUST KEEP YOUR OPINION TO YOURSELF AND RESPECT OTHER PEOPLE'S POINTS OF VIEW?"**

I thanked him for his question, then started to give him my answer. "May I tell you a story?" I asked. "Let's say I lived in an apartment on the tenth floor. Now, suppose you and I were old friends…"

"We're not old friends," he corrected me.

"Alright," I conceded. "Suppose you and I were *not* old friends. But suppose we were in my apartment on the tenth floor all the same, and suppose I mentioned that I was planning to paint my living room light green. What would you say? Maybe you'd say nothing. Or maybe you'd say, 'Well, Avi, I think light blue would be a much better color, but that's just my opinion and I respect your point of view.'"

"Is this monologue going anywhere?" my questioner cut in.

"It is," I promised. "Hear me out." He shrugged impatiently, and I went on. "Then, suppose I told you, 'By the way, I can fly.' You still might say nothing. Or, maybe you'd say, 'Well, I don't think so, but that's just my opinion, and I respect your point of view.' But then, suppose I said, 'No, wait, let me prove to you that I can fly.' Then, suppose I walked over to the window, opened it, and climbed out onto the ledge. We're not talking about colors of paint anymore. We're talking about life and death. Would you stay silent, would you tell me that you respect my point of view, or would you try to talk me off of the ledge?"

"If it were *you*," the man said, "I'd just let you jump."

WHY SHARE THE GOSPEL?

There are many personal stories in this book because I like telling stories, and I hope you'll like reading them. But this book isn't an autobiography, nor is this book about methodology. In other words, it's not a "how to" book. If anything, it's a "why," as in:

+ Why we mustn't be ashamed of sharing the good news in an open and direct fashion.

+ Why the forthright presentation of the gospel message always produces a wide range of fruit.

+ Why believers find it difficult to share the good news, despite the variety of fruit that always abounds.

+ Why nonbelievers often choose to walk away from the claims of the Messiah, even when they know or at least suspect in their hearts that His claims are true.

+ Why believers in the early centuries of our current era felt compelled to proclaim His message, regardless of the risks and costs, and what we can learn from that.

Finally, it's a book about why I believe that silence simply isn't an option.

By temperament, I'm actually a private person. True, I desire and appreciate affirmation as much as everyone else, and I'd never pass the test for joining a society of recluses. But I'll take reading over chatting, or a movie in a darkened and semi-deserted auditorium over a public sports match. And if friends get together for a game of Monopoly, I'd just as soon watch rather than play. I'll be the first person to admit that some news ought to remain private, especially if it's too personal, or self-indulgent or, even worse, just plain boring. But if the news we possess happens to be life-changing, universally relevant, and urgent, well then, we can't keep that news under wraps whether we're private people or not.

PEOPLE PERISH WHILE WE'RE SILENT

When it comes to the gospel, silence is not golden. Neither is it an effective evangelistic strategy, or even a biblically endorsed method of promoting the *message* of the good news. How can you further a message if you never state what that message is?

Perhaps most important of all, silence is not a genuine act of respect or love—not if silence allows the beloved to perish.

Jesus never loved us with a silent love. Yes, He performed many deeds that caught our attention. But as uncomfortable as it might be for believers to accept, Yeshua's ministry during the three years leading up to His death, resurrection, and ascension consisted first and foremost of a ministry of the spoken word. Because He loved us, He told us what we needed to hear, even though He knew how the majority of us would initially react. He had to speak; love compelled Him to speak.

And because He spoke, people heard, believed, and followed.

IT'S BECOME VERY POPULAR TO DISPARAGE AN OPEN AND CLEAR PRESENTATION OF THE LIFE-CHANGING MESSAGE OF THE GOSPEL. BUT WE MUST SHARE IT!

But let's be honest. It's become very popular to disparage an open and clear presentation of the gospel message to those who still need to hear it, even when that message is delivered in a sensitive and considerate fashion. As a result, those of us who've already heard and received that life-changing message find as many reasons as possible to refrain from sharing it with others. We're like people who've been rescued from a shipwreck. In joy over our deliverance, we decide to hold a great barbecue on the beach in honor of the lifeguards who pulled us out of the sea. We're so busy singing songs of deliverance and thanksgiving that we don't quite notice the hint of sadness on our rescuers' faces. Finally, one of us asks, "Is something wrong?" Then, a spokesperson for the lifeguards directs our focus back toward the sea. "We heard *your* cries," he says. "What about *theirs?*"

If you're not yet a follower of Yeshua (Jesus), then I hope you'll come away from this book with a better grasp of the message commonly called the *gospel* or the *good news*. I even hope you'll be moved to examine any reasons you might have for not giving that message an openhearted consideration. And I certainly hope you'll understand, if only a little, why we believers feel that we're doing you a greater disservice if we refrain from telling you what we think.

If you *are* a follower of Jesus, then I hope this book will encourage you and maybe even provoke you to speak openly about your faith with those who still need to hear.

Why is that so important?

Because we're not talking about what color to paint a room.

ONE

THAT DIRTY LITTLE WORD

Decades ago, I ministered for a while to an unsaved Jewish woman named Dora. She lived in a Jewish home for the aged. She was over one hundred years old, had a clear mind, and claimed to be a Marxist. In fact, she'd taken part in Lenin's October 1917 Revolution before immigrating to the United States sometime in the 1920s. She kept her room at the nursing home in good Soviet order. The only sprawl came from socialist publications that she liberally strewed about. But despite her political leanings, she had a strong Jewish identity and a genuine interest in Jesus. So she welcomed me very warmly whenever I came by to talk with her about the "dialectics" of faith.

However, she had a problem with me. One day, she said, "Avi, I know what you believe, but I don't really know who or what you are. What are you, Avi? What do you do?"

I shrugged. "Well, Dora, I have discussions about Jesus with people like you. I write articles. I organize meetings. I hand out literature on the streets."

Suddenly, a look of total comprehension flashed across her face. "Ahh," she exhaled. "You're a provocateur."

I nodded and smiled. "That's right, Dora. I'm a provocateur."

BEING A PROVOCATEUR FOR JESUS

Generally speaking, we don't view the words "provoke" and "provocation" in a very positive light. We think of them as *dirty* words—and for good reason. In biblical times, we Jews repeatedly provoked the Lord to anger by following after the false gods of the gentiles. But there's a sense in which provocation can be seen as something proper and good. Paul alludes to that sense in the eleventh chapter of his letter to the Romans, when he speaks of provoking us, his fellow Jews, to jealousy, so that we might come to faith in the Lord.

> THERE'S A DIFFERENCE BETWEEN NEEDLING PEOPLE TO GET UNDER THEIR SKIN AND PASSIONATELY IMPLORING THEM TO WRESTLE WITH GOSPEL TRUTHS.

Context is everything, of course. There's a difference between needling people just for the sake of getting under their skin and passionately imploring a person to wrestle with what you have to say. Biblical provocation arises from that earnest, second type of plea.

A number of features make up what we might easily call *a biblically provocative testimony*. In fact, quite a few of those features can be found clustered together in one particular passage of Scripture—the fortieth chapter of the book of Isaiah. But, oddly enough, many people fail to associate the first of those features with an upfront and unashamed declaration of the good news. That feature is compassion. A biblically provocative testimony is grounded in God's measureless compassion for the lost.

> **A BIBLICALLY PROVOCATIVE TESTIMONY IS GROUNDED IN GOD'S MEASURELESS COMPASSION FOR THE LOST.**

The Isaiah passage begins:

"Comfort, comfort My people," says your God. "Speak kindly to Jerusalem; and call out to her, that her warfare has ended, that her guilt has been removed, that she has received of the LORD's hand double for all her sins."

(Isaiah 40:1–2)

Taken together, those three exhortations—to comfort, to speak kindly, and to call out— encapsulate one of the most extravagant characteristics of the Lord: His infinite and burning compassion for the lost. A biblically provocative testimony wells up from that very compassion. It's the same compassion Yeshua felt for the crowd of people who desperately ran ahead of His boat when He and the twelve apostles headed off for a secluded place and a time of rest. (See Mark 6:31–33.) We're told, *"When Jesus went ashore, He saw a large crowd, and He felt compassion for them"* (verse 34)—so much so that He delayed the apostles' time of rest and spent the entire day teaching the crowd instead.

Why such a strong compassion? The text explains: *"Because they were like sheep without a shepherd."*

SHEEP NEED A SHEPHERD

I grew up in New York City, and as a child, I knew nothing about sheep. But later, I built a friendship with a man who had spent his youth on a ranch in rural Texas. He told me that sheep aren't very smart. They can't find their own food or water, and they don't even know enough to seek shelter in the midst of a deadly blizzard. My friend also told me that sheep are completely defenseless. They can't run very fast, and they have no teeth or claws with which to protect themselves from predators. Without a shepherd, sheep die either from the elements, from starvation, or from the wolves.

When Jesus looked upon the crowd, what kind of people did He see? Were they smart or ignorant? Were they wealthy or poor? Were they upright or ungodly? It doesn't matter. Jesus saw only one kind of people: dying people. *"He felt compassion for them because they were like sheep without a shepherd; and He began to teach them many things"* (Mark 6:34).

COMPASSION FUELED PAUL'S PASSION

Have you ever wondered what might have fueled the apostle Paul's provocative, relentless pursuit of the salvation of us, his kinsman according to the flesh, even though many of us sought his death? Undoubtedly, he saw us through the Savior's eyes and experienced the same intense compassion that resided in the Savior's heart. That compassion isn't natural. It's supernatural, and it's given to those who ask. But once it's bestowed, it cannot be contained.

I know a woman named Paula. One morning during an outreach in Budapest, she asked the Lord to grant her the grace to see people the way He saw them, to taste just a portion of the compassion that He felt for the people she was about to encounter on the streets. Later, she told me what happened. When she stepped outside, she found herself so overwhelmed at the sight of the people that she sat down on the curb and wept. That morning, Paula spoke with every person she met and introduced four of them to the Lord.

A biblically provocative testimony wells up from a desire that all may hear so that none might perish. A biblically provocative testimony mirrors God's burning compassion for the lost and offers a genuine word of comfort and hope.

> **A BIBLICALLY PROVOCATIVE TESTIMONY OFFERS A GENUINE WORD OF COMFORT AND HOPE.**

God tells us through Isaiah, *"Comfort, comfort My people… her guilt has been removed."*

Leslie was twenty-five years old, and she was dying. The doctors had given her about a month to live. I sat at the foot of her bed, and we talked about unimportant matters for a few minutes. At one point, she asked, more out of courtesy than anything else, "So how are things with you?"

I smiled wanly, "Life's a tempest."

"Really?" she asked with mock interest. "What tempests are *you* dealing with?"

"They're nothing compared to yours," I said, softly and honestly. Then I asked, "So how can I be praying for you?"

HEALING IS SUCH A MINOR MIRACLE

Apparently, my question gave her the emotional permission to drop her stoic front. She lowered her head and sobbed very deeply. I sat quietly and let her weep. After a short while, she stared rather sharply at me and asked point blank, "Can your Jesus heal me?"

I thought for a moment. Then I said, "Yes, if He wants to. But that's such a minor miracle."

Leslie looked surprised. "How is that a *minor* miracle?" she asked. "I'm *dying*."

I answered her, softly but directly. "It's a minor miracle because you're still going to die. Everyone dies. But there's a *major* miracle that He'll always perform whenever we ask."

"What miracle?"

"He'll forgive our sins, and He'll grant us the gift of eternal life."

I explained the good news. There *is* hope, and there *is* rescue, if we'll seize it. God waits for us to acknowledge that we've been wrong so that He can forgive and rescue us from the hopelessness to which we've succumbed.

"One way or the other, Jesus wants to carry you through this turmoil," I told Leslie. "If you ask Him to forgive you, He'll forgive you. He'll stay with you now, and He'll bring you to Himself whenever your life finally ends. If you ask Him to heal you as well, maybe He'll say yes, and maybe you'll live another sixty years. Or maybe He'll say no, and maybe you'll die in a month. But if you die in a month, I'll be jealous."

Once again, my words startled her. "Why would you be jealous?" she asked.

"Because you'll get to see Him before I do, and that's not entirely fair."

So, Leslie prayed with me. First, we asked the Lord to forgive her, and He did. Then we asked Him to heal her, and He didn't. She died within the month.

Leslie is a lot happier right now than either you or me. She's rejoicing in the very presence of the Lord. You and I are still trying to keep our footing in the midst of our tempests.

No one could offer Leslie any hope. Neither the doctors, nor the nurses, nor the therapists, nor even the rabbi who regularly stopped in to visit patients at the hospital. At best, friends offered her meaningless platitudes, words of sterile consolation. And while the doctors just wrote her off, the attending nurses simply did their best to make her *comfortable*.

Leslie needed much more.

A biblically provocative testimony offers a genuine word of comfort and a genuine word of hope by declaring a single message: the gospel.

> **A BIBLICALLY PROVOCATIVE TESTIMONY DECLARES A SINGLE MESSAGE: THE GOSPEL.**

Later in that same chapter from Isaiah, God commands His messengers to deliver the good news. (See Isaiah 40:9.) It's the good news that our warfare with God can be ended and our iniquity can be removed. (See verse 2.) It's the good news that though we're His enemies, we can be reconciled to God through the sacrifice of His Son. (See Romans 5:10.) That's a provocative message; we don't like being told that we're at war with God. But we are.

SLAVES TO OUR NATURE

We're born with disobedient, rebellious hearts, and we practice that rebellion against God all of our lives. As a result of our waywardness, we spend the journey of our lives in pointless wandering. Nothing satisfies us; every endeavor becomes an exercise of chasing after the wind. (See Ecclesiastes.) And even if we long to change our lives, we can't. We're enslaved to our nature no matter how many seminars we attend, or how many well-intentioned resolutions we make. Finally, we die, and if we haven't received Jesus as our Savior, we enter a conscious eternity cut off from God—an existence so horrific that Isaiah can only describe it with nightmarish images, calling it a place where *"their worm will not die and their fire will not be extinguished"* (Isaiah 66:24).

We need to be rescued. We need to be freed from the power that a disobedient heart exercises over our daily lives, and we need to be delivered from the ultimate and eternal divorce from God that our rebellion deserves. Because of His limitless love for us, this is precisely what God set out to do.

When Yeshua died on the cross, He took upon Himself the punishment of God that I deserve and that you deserve. As He hung on a cross, dying, He cried out, *"My God, My God, why have You forsaken Me?"* (Matthew 27:46; Mark 15:34). Why those words from Psalm 22:1? Because in that moment, He experienced the agony of being utterly forsaken by the Father. And He screamed.

That should have been my scream. And that should have been your scream. But He loves us so passionately that He willingly endured that agony on our behalf so that we might never have to utter that scream. Then He rose from the dead so that He can pardon us as soon as we come to our senses and repent.

YESHUA RESCUES US FROM BANISHMENT

When we ask Him to forgive us, He rescues us from the eternal banishment of God that we deserve, and He places His own Holy Spirit within us so that we can live the kind of lives that please and glorify Him. Now we can say with King David, *"Goodness and mercy shall follow me all the days of my life, and I shall dwell in the house of the Lord forever"* (Psalm 23:6 ESV). That goodness, mercy, and gift of eternal life in the house of the Lord become our own the moment we trust what Jesus accomplished for us and repent of our sin. This is the message that a biblically provocative testimony unashamedly puts forth.

> ONE SHOULD NEVER BE ASHAMED TO SHARE THE BIBLICALLY PROVOCATIVE TESTIMONY THAT JESUS CAN GIVE US ETERNAL LIFE.

Once, in Essen, Germany, a young punk rocker named Sara approached me with her eyes glued to the words on my shirt: *Juden für Jesus*. She stopped about an arm's length away from me, cautiously stretched out her hand, and then slowly glided her fingers across the words on my chest.

"Can this be true?" she asked softly.

"Do you want it to be true?" I asked back.

Her eyes began to fill with tears. "I want it to be true so much," she said.

"It's true," I told her. Later that week, Sara gave her heart to the Lord.

In Isaiah 40:9, we're told, "*Go up on a high mountain*" to spread the good news. In the same fashion, Yeshua told His disciples:

> *You are the light of the world. A city set on a hill cannot be hidden; nor do people light a lamp and put it under a basket, but on a lampstand, and it gives light to all who are in the house. Your light must shine before people in such a way that they may see your good works, and glorify your Father who is in heaven.* (Matthew 5:14–16)

When John the Baptist came out of the Judean desert, he wore a garment of camel's hair and a leather belt. His clothes symbolized a calling; John claimed to be a messenger in the order of God's Old Testament prophets. And to make certain that everyone understood that claim, he described himself by using the very words that we find in Isaiah 40. When asked who he was, John replied, "*I am the voice of one crying out in the wilderness, 'Make straight the way of the Lord,' as the prophet Isaiah said*" (John 1:23 ESV; compare Isaiah 40:3).

By wearing those distinctive clothes, John deliberately called attention to his presence and his purpose, even before he spoke a single word. By his very clothing, he declared, "Take note of me!"

TAKING A COURAGEOUS, NOTICEABLE STAND

In the very beginning of the Jews for Jesus movement, we were—and still are—very outspoken about who we are (Jews) and who we are for (Jesus). Our commitment to "outing" ourselves and putting forth a visible, provocative testimony accomplished many goals. It expressed our solidarity with our people, even if some or many of them wished to cast us off. It demonstrated a determination to take a courageous stand, whether we felt especially courageous or not. It made the statement that we belonged to a discernable movement, amassing numbers and momentum.

Our visibility inspired, even provoked, non-Jewish believers to take an equally forthright stand for the faith. Other believers in Jesus thought, *If these Jews can openly proclaim their faith without fear or shame, then what's stopping us?*

Skeptics would chide us, saying things like, "Jews for Jesus? Isn't that like vegetarians for meat or sex fiends for virginity?" But the sense of dissonance that our visible presence provoked couldn't help but have an immediate impact. We arrested attention for the sake of the gospel wherever we went. No one turned a blind eye or a deaf ear. Everyone took note. Seekers could easily find us because of our accessibility, while the opposition we encountered only served to call greater attention to the statement we were putting out.

In a word, our visibility created a no-lose situation wherever we went.

During a street campaign in Berlin, Germany, I watched as a young Palestinian women caught sight of the words *Jews for Jesus* in German and Hebrew on the shirt of a young colleague of mine from Israel. The women flew into a rage. "I want Israel to be erased!" she screamed. "I want *Israelis* to be erased!"

My coworker, Dani, placed his palm on his chest and asked, "Do you want *this* Israeli to be erased?" The softness of his voice caught her off guard, and she fell silent. Dani spoke into the pause. "You and I aren't enemies," he told her. "We're family. That's why we pray for you as much as we pray for our own." A brief back-and-forth exchange followed his words. The woman found it hard to talk and even harder to listen, but she did both. At the end of the conversation, she took Dani's gospel literature, stared at it for a moment, and then put it into her pocket and walked on.

Someday, Dani and I will know the final outcome of that encounter. But for now, we know this much: she heard the most important message that she'll ever hear in her life. The opportunity arose because Dani had made himself visible.

Am I advocating that all believers wear distinctive clothing? No. Am I advocating that all believers "come out of the closet" in one way or another? Yes.

CAN PEOPLE BE SECRET BELIEVERS?

The visibility built into the act of biblical provocation raises some uncomfortable questions. Can people really be secret believers? If yes, then can they remain secret believers indefinitely? If all of us are called to be witnesses in some way, then how can we fulfill that call if we keep our faith completely and permanently under wraps?

We can't. The timing and manner of our open identification with the Lord must be an individual matter. And we need to weigh and accept the severity of the consequences we'll face, especially when our open identification endangers our very lives. But ultimately, that open identification must take place, regardless of the cost. All of us must, in some manner, get up on a high mountain and let our light shine.

A biblically provocative testimony requires us to get up on the mountain, to mount the uncomfortable platform of open association with the Lord. We must stand upon the Rock of our salvation, not just theologically, but visibly as well.

And once we step onto that plateau, we find ourselves shouldering another crucial responsibility—the responsibility to speak.

> **A BIBLICALLY PROVOCATIVE TESTIMONY POSSESSES A VOICE THAT IS WILLING TO LOUDLY DECLARE AN OPEN ASSOCIATION WITH THE LORD.**

I found myself alone on Christmas Day in Budapest in 2013. The staff had the day off, and for some reason, my wife Ruth was away, perhaps at a women's conference—I don't really recall. I decided to travel into the center of the city, just to get out of our empty flat. I didn't expect to encounter anyone on the streets; it was, after all, Christmas Day. But I took a few hundred of my tracts with me just the same. When I exited the metro at the Blaha Lujza station and walked back up to the street level, I came upon a sight that I hardly expected to see. About five hundred men, women, and children, mostly Roma (Gypsies) and "street people," stood dutifully in line, waiting for a make-shift holiday soup kitchen to open up. A small combo played traditional Christmas melodies. Good-looking young men and women were readying the soup and slicing the bread.

But one piece of this idyllic scene marred the entire picture. The soup kitchen organizers had hung a banner between two trees, wishing people happy holidays from the local chapter of Hare Krishna, a Hindu sect.

Suddenly, I understood why I'd felt compelled to bring along my tracts.

RAISE YOUR VOICE FORCEFULLY

Believers in Jesus aren't the only people who can care for people's needs. But believers *are* the only people who can offer God's message of eternal life.

Isaiah says, *"Raise your voice forcefully…Say to the cities of Judah, 'Here is your God!'"* (Isaiah 40:9).

Do you remember the story about Moses and the burning bush? We know from the biblical account that the Lord captured Moses's attention through a very visible manifestation of His presence.

> *The angel of the* Lord *appeared to him in a blazing fire from the midst of a bush; and he looked, and behold, the bush was burning with fire, yet the bush was not being consumed.* (Exodus 3:2)

Not only did the Lord arrest Moses's attention, He provoked his curiosity as well. Moses told himself, *"I must turn aside and see this marvelous sight, why the bush is not burning up!"* (verse 3).

Moses climbed the mountain, and then God's voice called out to him from the midst of the bush. In other words, God *spoke.* The rest of Exodus 3 and most of chapter 4 record the monumental, history-changing conversation that took place.

But what if no conversation had occurred? Would Moses have been able to glean just from the miraculous sight of the burning bush that God wanted him to confront Pharaoh and deliver us from our bondage in Egypt? No. Without the conversation, the purpose of the sign meant nothing. God's presence in the bush required an explanation. God's message for Moses needed a voice.

And so does the gospel message. It must be verbalized if people are to understand what God wants from them.

Of course, *verbal* and *vocal* aren't necessarily the same thing. Communication may be verbal, but it might not be audible at all. A message can be written, signed, or depicted in any number of nonvocal ways. But whether it's carried by sound, sign, image, or text, it must be communicated through words or symbols that convey concrete meaning and sense.

In recent years, it's become popular for some believers to advocate a silent, nonverbal testimony of lifestyle in which people live out the gospel message rather than share it through any words. A quote ascribed to Saint Francis of Assisi is often cited for support: "Preach the gospel at all times. Use words if necessary."

There are at least two problems with this quote. The first is the fact that St. Francis never uttered those words. According to the Franciscans themselves, that famous quote cannot be found either in Francis' writing or in any of his early biographies. But more importantly, the alleged quote reveals a basic misunderstanding of the very nature of the gospel message itself—namely, that the good news is a content-driven message.

In a sense, there are two types of messages in the realm of communication: those that are driven forward by content, and those that are driven forward by conduct. In many ways, parental love is a *conduct*-driven message. Children understand that they're loved because of their parents' conduct long before they understand the meaning of the words of love that their parents shower upon them. But a *content*-driven message consists of specific information that must be shared.

> **THE GOOD NEWS IS A CONTENT-DRIVEN MESSAGE OF SPECIFIC INFORMATION THAT MUST BE SHARED.**

Suppose I must fly from Budapest to Warsaw tomorrow morning on Europa Airlines flight 123, leaving from Budapest at 09:40 hours. I have to check in either online or at the terminal, and I have to arrive at the right airport on the right date and at the right time. I must pass through security control and get to the correct gate no later than ten minutes before the flight departs. And for the sake of drama, let's say that my life depends upon my being on that particular flight. Can someone's lifestyle or conduct bring me to the right airport at the right time on the right date? No, not unless that conduct includes the verbal communication of the content that I need to know.

The gospel message is a content-driven message—and our lives depend on it. It must be communicated through words that make sense to those who read or hear this message. Otherwise, it has no meaning.

Have you noticed that when the Bible commands men and women to communicate God's message to others, that command is almost always expressed with verbs such as *speak, say, tell, proclaim,* and *declare?* Paul himself reminds us, *"Faith comes from hearing, and hearing by the word of Christ"* (Romans 10:17). If a testimony of good deeds were good enough, if lifestyle alone were sufficient for communicating the good news, then the Lord wouldn't have bothered to give us His Word.

PEOPLE NEED MORE THAN GOOD WORKS

But didn't Jesus tell us, *"Your light must shine before people in such a way that they may see your good works, and glorify your Father who is in heaven"* (Matthew 5:16)? Yes, He did. However, this exhortation presumes that people will connect the conduct of good works to the content of the message that gave rise to those good works. Without the message, people will interpret the meaning of those good works in whatever way they want. That hardly leads to the Father being glorified.

But isn't there a relationship between the content of the message and the conduct of the one who carries it? Yes, a very crucial relationship. Conduct *brackets* the content. The Lord may use our conduct to draw people to the content, and He may use our conduct to confirm that the content is true. But the content must be present and put forth.

Perhaps one of the most moving examples of this bracketing principle is recorded in Mark 2, when Yeshua healed the paralytic man. Four men came to Him, carrying a friend on a stretcher. They came in anticipation of a healing. But before performing the miracle, Jesus made an audacious claim. He turned to the man and said, *"Son, your sins are forgiven"* (verse

5). The text itself goes on to explain precisely why He then performed the miracle of healing the man. He told His opponents who stood nearby, "*So that you may know that the Son of Man has authority on earth to forgive sins*" (Mark 2:10).

Had Jesus merely healed the man, no one in the crowd would have understood from the act alone that Jesus had the authority to forgive sins. His silence would have given them the freedom to give the miracle whatever meaning they chose. In their wonder, they might have revered Jesus as a remarkable miracle worker, but nothing more.

Jesus wanted more—much more. He wanted them to know that He had the power to forgive their sins, and He wanted them to know that He possessed a prerogative that His detractors correctly acknowledged as belonging to God alone. In short, Jesus wanted the people to grapple with who He is as well as what He can do. First, He spoke. Then, He performed a lesser miracle of healing to confirm that a greater miracle of forgiveness had taken place. He used a miracle that they could see to confirm the reality of a miracle that He declared, but the latter remained hidden from their sight.

Jesus confirmed the claims of His lips with the conduct of His life. And so must we. Yes, our lives should stand as living proof that what we believe and what we declare is true. But we still need to declare and explain. We must give verbal testimony to what we know to be true.

> **A BIBLICALLY PROVOCATIVE TESTIMONY REQUIRES COURAGE TO DECLARE WHAT WE KNOW TO BE TRUE.**

To be honest, I don't remember feeling either especially frightened or especially courageous. I simply stared at the long line of people bordering the perimeter of Red Square in Moscow. It was May 1990, and the Soviet Union was falling apart. My wife and I had brought a probe team to the USSR to explore the possibility of starting a ministry there. When we came to Red Square, we saw a line of a thousand or more people, dutifully waiting for a turn to enter Lenin's Mausoleum. They'd come to pay homage to a dead revolutionary. They needed to hear about a living Redeemer.

I started to hand out literature to the people standing quietly in line, but I didn't get a chance to share very much. Within just a few moments, a Soviet guard grabbed the material from my hands and demanded in Russian, "*Shto eta takoi!?*"—that is, "What is this?" My colleague, Liza Terini, rushed to my aid. "It's good news," she answered warmly in Russian. "Read it, please." The guard quickly scanned the words on the paper, smiled sardonically, cast a cautious glance over his shoulder, and then positioned the five of us throughout Red Square so that we could distribute the literature more quickly and efficiently.

DO NOT BE AFRAID!

Hundreds of times throughout the Bible, God tells us—through His prophets, angels, or some other means—to choose courage. As early as Genesis 15, we read:

> The word of the LORD came to Abram in a vision, saying, "Do not fear, Abram, I am a shield to you; your reward shall be very great." (Genesis 15:1)

We need to deal honestly with three facts about our fear. First, fear is pervasive, even after we've believed. Paul told his son in the faith, Timothy, that God has not given us a spirit of fear. (See 2 Timothy 1:7.) But Paul's exhortation itself speaks of the lingering reality of fear in Timothy's life. Fear doesn't want to let go. It clings to us, like a chronic disease.

Second, though fear lingers and tugs, we mustn't succumb to its pull. We're repeatedly commanded not to submit to fear, but to oppose it with our faith in God. We can obey that commandment more readily if we remember that "fearless" doesn't necessarily describe our feelings; it describes our actions. Even when we feel frightened, we can still act in a courageous way.

And third, we need to understand that we commit a severe error whenever we choose a course of action that's based on our fear of any opposition that we may face. By definition, acting courageously means that we choose to do what's correct in God's sight, regardless of what it might cost us when we obey.

What if Moses had failed to muster the courage to confront Pharaoh and demand that he let God's people go? (See Exodus 5:1.) What if Nathan had failed to muster the courage to confront David over his adultery and murder? (See 2 Samuel 12:9.) These two incidents ended well for the messengers who found the courage to speak. But that's not always the case. It didn't end well for Isaiah, Jeremiah, Stephen, or James.

The Bible and post-biblical history are filled with the examples of men and women who died for acting with biblical courage. To this day, I don't know why the five of us on that Moscow probe team in 1990 weren't hauled away, never to be heard from again. Acting with godly courage might not have a *happy ending.*

But that doesn't matter. Yeshua has called us to proclaim the good news, so *speaking out* with courage is what matters.

BE COURAGEOUS, NOT RECKLESS

Granted, there is a difference between godly courage and reckless, worldly showmanship. Reckless behavior seeks to garner praise and adoration for ourselves. Courage seeks to do the *right thing.* Knowing what's right is the key. Certainly, there will be times when the right course is a prudent, cautious way forward. But not always. And we'll never determine the right course of action if we're committed to avoiding all danger at any cost.

God never promised us the absence of danger, just the assurance of ultimate security in the midst of any danger we may confront. *"Who will separate us from the love of Christ? Will tribulation, or trouble, or persecution, or famine, or nakedness, or danger, or sword?"* (Romans 8:35). No.

Nowhere are we commanded to avoid danger or flee from its presence because of fear. Just imagine how much further the gospel might be advanced through our labors and in our very lives if we cultivated the habit of pressing on in the fear of the Lord, rather than falling back because of our fear of man.

> **A BIBLICALLY PROVOCATIVE TESTIMONY HIGHLIGHTS THE GOSPEL'S RELEVANCE TO A LOST AND HOPELESS WORLD.**

"Behold *your* God," Isaiah cries. (See Isaiah 40:9 ESV.)

I grew up in a typical Jewish home. We weren't against Jesus, just wary. My family, friends, and I knew that He was one of our own…but that was about it. And while we didn't know the gospel message, we did know Christian history as it relates to us Jews. The Crusades. The Inquisition. The pogroms. The church's silence during the Holocaust. We knew what had been done to us throughout the centuries by people who claimed to be His followers, but who despised the very people—*His* people!—whom He loves and longs to save.

Long before postmodernism gave us the accommodating phrase, "That's *your* truth," we kept Jesus at bay by pointing out that whoever He might be, He simply wasn't for us. "Jesus is fine for you, but we're Jewish," we would explain. Those two words, "We're Jewish," conveyed it all: Jesus didn't apply to us. He wasn't relevant.

A biblically provocative testimony will invariably make the claim that Jesus *is* relevant to everyone, Jew and non-Jew alike. His message becomes a compelling issue that we cannot ignore. We have to deal with what He said and who He claimed to be. He *is* relevant to *all* of us because He is *our* God.

THE GOSPEL *IS* RELEVANT

Sometimes we mistakenly talk about the need to make the gospel relevant. I know what we mean, but we should guard ourselves against sloppy terminology that actually devalues the good news. To say that we need to make the gospel relevant is like saying that we need to make the gospel true. We don't need to do either—because the gospel *is* relevant, and the gospel *is* true. Rather, we need to find the best ways to help people understand that the gospel is relevant, true, and necessary for their lives. That's a matter of methodology, of finding the right methods and means that accurately communicate the message and highlight its relevance to the lives of those who hear it.

Methodologies will always change. But the message never changes, nor does its relevance ever fade.

A biblically provocative testimony denies us the luxury of dismissing the gospel as irrelevant. We're compelled to behold our God. *"Behold...Behold...Behold..."* (Isaiah 40:9–10 ESV).

> ## A BIBLICALLY PROVOCATIVE TESTIMONY WILL ALWAYS CALL FOR A RESPONSE.

Just a few scant days after our deliverance from Egypt, we faced a horrifying and seemingly insurmountable challenge. Pharaoh's army and six hundred of his choicest chariots were racing down upon us, and they weren't coming out to talk. In an absolute panic, we cried out to Moses. But the words we hurled at him sounded less like a plea for help and more like a bitter, terror-filled wail of hopeless regret:

> *They said to Moses, "Is it because there were no graves in Egypt that you have taken us away to die in the wilderness? Why have you dealt with us in this way, bringing us out of Egypt?"*   (Exodus 14:11)

In a moment of what can only be described as God-given grace and patience, Moses overlooked our accusation and said, *"Do not fear! Stand by and see [behold] the salvation of the LORD, which He will perform for you today"* (verse 13). Then, upon God's command, Moses stretched out his shepherd's rod and caused the Red Sea to part in two.

We know how the incident ended, of course. The children of Israel crossed the sea on dry ground and arrived safely on the other side. But when the Egyptians pursued us, God collapsed the waters upon them, and they drowned.

What if we'd responded to the parted sea in a different fashion? What if we'd merely taken note of the means of salvation in front of us, but had failed to step out in faith onto the dry riverbed? We would have died. We had to respond with faith by moving out. A biblically provocative testimony calls for people to respond.

God has never been in the business of simply putting out information for the sake of *keeping people in the loop*. Rather, His intention and desire have always been to elicit a response—specifically, the response of coming back to Him. He calls out, *"Turn to Me and be saved, all the ends of the earth"* (Isaiah 45:22). *Turning* is our response to His call. *Saving* is His response to our turning back to Him.

Paul explained to the Athenians, *"God is now proclaiming to mankind that all people everywhere are to repent"* (Acts 17:30). God's intention hasn't changed. A biblically provocative testimony calls us to respond in faith.

> GOD'S INTENTION HASN'T CHANGED. A BIBLICALLY PROVOCATIVE TESTIMONY CALLS US TO RESPOND IN FAITH.

An honest and up-front offering of our faith will invariably strike many as provocative, which can be especially discomforting for those of us who possess a more introverted temperament. I often marvel over the fact that God chose to call me into a ministry that has always prioritized an open presentation of the good news. But I marvel even more over the grace that He's always given me in every uncomfortable situation. And I've discovered to my delight that a steady, gentle, and even self-effacing voice in an awkward situation can be the most effective voice of all. But this shouldn't really surprise us if we remember that gentleness is a manifestation of the fruit of His Spirit, and that "*a soft answer turns away wrath*" (Proverbs 15:1 ESV).

"Soft" and "silent" are not synonymous. Neither are "sincere" and "strident." We can be quiet *and* compelling. But whether we're loud or soft, we mustn't be ashamed. We simply need to remember that an unashamed stance will always strike someone as provocative, no matter how gentle our posture and words might be. That truth actually gives us private types something of an edge. Our temperaments allow us to be clear but not overbearing. By nature, we're happy to let the message itself do all the heavy work.

THE GREATEST PROVOCATEUR

Without a doubt, the greatest provocateur was, and *is*, the Messiah Himself, Yeshua, Jesus of Nazareth.

He provoked us by the way He invaded history. To be born of a virgin guaranteed that His life would always be scandalized by doubts about the propriety of His conception.

He provoked us with the company He kept and the people He called—not just fishermen, tax collectors, adulterers, and prostitutes, but *Galileans*! (Located far north of Jerusalem, Galilee was considered to be the most pagan of the Jewish provinces.)

He provoked us with the miracles He performed. He healed on the Sabbath. He cleansed a leper by touching him without making Himself unclean. He restored a blind man's sight by creating living tissue out of clay.

He provoked us with the manner in which He taught, citing no authority other than His own.

He provoked us by unilaterally forgiving sins, a prerogative reserved for God.

He provoked us by raising people from the dead without asking God either for permission or assistance.

He provoked us by calling Himself *"Lord of the Sabbath"* (Matthew 12:8), *"the bread of life...come down from heaven"* (John 6:35, 38), the One to whom the Law and Prophets point (see Luke 24:44), and the only way to the Father (see John 14:6).

He provoked us by making the unmistakable and unacceptable claim, *"I and the Father are one"* (John 10:30).

Once we allow ourselves to look candidly at the Gospel accounts, we're forced to ask: Is there anything, anywhere, in the claims and conduct of Yeshua that *isn't* provocative?

Jesus provokes us today. He provokes those of us who haven't yet believed and repented to deal with His claims and His works, regardless of what it might cost, and regardless of what people might think. He provokes those of us who *have* believed and repented to stand openly for Him without fear or shame, to put the obligation of following Him above every other commitment and relationship, to die to ourselves and live only for Him. If anyone stands guilty of being a provocateur, it's Jesus.

Perhaps provocation isn't such a dirty word after all.

What happens when we present the gospel in a loving but direct, forthright, even provocative manner? Quite a lot. Let me tell you a story...

TWO

THE LITTLE OLD MAN ON 57TH STREET

(OR WHY I WASTE MY TIME PROCLAIMING THE GOOD NEWS)

From the mid-1960s through the early 1970s, a genuine revival swept across North America. That should come as no surprise; those were turbulent years. The war in Vietnam, the racial confrontations and strife, and the killing of our heroes, from the Kennedys to Martin Luther King Jr. Our disillusionment with the Great Society, coupled with a profound distrust of authorities, provoked a demand for change—a demand that ranged from calls for reform to cries for revolution.

In the midst of it all, revival broke out.

The news journal *Time Magazine* dubbed it *the Jesus Revolution*. Millions of young men and women surrendered their lives to Jesus during that feverish time. New missions and church movements sprang up, radical and counterculture, like the people who were coming to faith. At the same time, existing ministries found themselves reinvigorated and flushed with waves of new seekers. People desperately wanted answers and hope. Both were found in the hope of Israel, the Messiah Yeshua.

Talk of God was everywhere—in the secular press, on late-night TV talk shows, and certainly out on the streets.

> **THE LITTLE OLD MAN ON 57TH STREET WAS PASSING OUT PIECES OF PAPER QUOTING JOHN 3:16—THE FIRST GOSPEL SEED THAT GOD SOWED INTO MY LIFE.**

I was sixteen years old in 1967, and I lived in New York City. One day, while walking down 57th Street across from the entrance to Central Park South, I noticed a disheveled little old man, hovering against the side of a building, clutching a paper bag in his hand. As people passed by, he darted his free hand into the bag, pulled out a scrap of paper, and blindly thrust it into the air in front of him.

I watched him and thought, "This is so weird, it must have something to do with God." So, I moved close enough to put myself in his path, and then I took a scrap of paper when his jab invaded the space in front of my chest.

I guessed right. The paper had something to do with God. The words on the paper stated in the old Kings James Version of the Bible, *"For God so loved the world, that he gave his only begotten Son, that whosoever believeth in him should not perish, but have everlasting life"* (John 3:16 KJV). Somehow, I knew that the quote came from the New Testament. As a joke, I decided to memorize those words, so that I could boast to my friends in school that I knew a verse from that *other* book—the one we Jews didn't read.

To my knowledge, this verse is the first gospel seed that God sowed into my life. Did it have any effect? It did. I'm still talking about the incident more than fifty years later.

RUNNING INTO JEWS FOR JESUS

Jump ahead with me eight years, to July 1975. Once again, I happened to be walking down a New York City street—this time, Eighth Avenue, in front of the Port Authority bus terminal. I walked with a friend of mine who'd already become a believer in Jesus. But that didn't bother me because she was a gentile, and gentiles, I thought, are *supposed* to believe in Jesus.

Suddenly, my friend said, "Avi, look!" I stared ahead, in the direction of her nod. Then I froze. Just a few feet away from me stood a young man wearing a T-shirt emblazoned with the words, "Jews for Jesus." As I gawked, dumbfounded and angry, my friend walked up to the young man and took one of the pamphlets that he was handing out. Then she came back to me.

As far as I could tell, this man embodied the ultimate act of cultural treason. I turned to my friend and snarled, "Someone should tell this idiot that you can't be Jewish and believe in Jesus."

"Tell him yourself," she parried. Then she took my hand and placed the pamphlet into my palm. The title read, *"Jews Should Not Believe in Jesus...Unless..."* When I opened the pamphlet, I found a list of prophecies from the Hebrew Scriptures, the Old Testament, that *clearly* pointed to Jesus.

> **AFTER READING ABOUT THE MESSIANIC THEME IN THE SCRIPTURES, STARTING IN GENESIS, I REALIZED THAT I WAS STANDING ON THE THRESHOLD OF FAITH.**

Jump ahead another year and a half to December 1976. A different Christian friend gave me a book as a Hanukkah gift—*The Messianic Hope*, written by a British-born Jewish believer in Jesus named Dr. Arthur Kac.[1] The book traced the development of the messianic theme in the Scriptures, starting in Genesis, traveling through key prophetic passages like Micah 5:2 and Isaiah 53, and ending with the career of Jesus of Nazareth, detailed in the New Testament. After finishing the book, I remember writing in a journal, "I'm standing on the threshold of faith." I'd discovered that what Jesus told some of my ancestors was true. *"If you believed Moses, you would believe Me; for he wrote about Me"* (John 5:46). I knew it was just a matter of time.

On March 14, 1977, I told Jesus I was sorry. I prayed, asked Him to forgive me, and promised to follow Him.

Ten years. Seed, upon seed, upon seed. And none of it was wasted.

---

1. Arthur W. Kac, *The Messianic Hope: A Divine Solution for the Human Problem* (Grand Rapids, MI: Baker Books, 1975).

GOD'S UNEQUIVOCAL GUARANTEE

In Isaiah 55:10–11, God emphatically declares:

For as the rain and the snow come down from heaven, and do not return there without watering the earth and making it produce and sprout, and providing seed to the sower and bread to the eater; so will **My word** *be which goes out of My mouth; it* **will not return to Me empty**, *without accomplishing what I desire, and without succeeding in the purpose for which I sent it.*

That passage contains one of God's strongest promises to those of us who take up His commandment to share the good news. The proclamation of the gospel message always produces fruit.

Isaiah isn't the only inspired spokesperson to give us God's guarantee about the fruitfulness of our proclamation. David told us:

Those who sow in tears shall harvest with joyful shouting. One who goes here and there weeping, carrying his bag of seed, shall indeed come again with a shout of joy, bringing his sheaves with him.   (Psalm 126:5–6)

And the apostle Paul echoed that confidence when he told the Corinthians that our labors in the Lord are never in vain. (See 1 Corinthians 15:58.)

GOD'S WORD BRINGS *HIS* FRUIT

Regardless of the method—whether through a tract or a song, through a sermon, a podcast, or a one-on-one conversation at a sidewalk café—whenever we share the message in an accurate and truthful manner, God's Word never returns void.

But there's a catch, right there in Isaiah 55:11. The fruit that God's Word brings forth is the fruit that *God* wants it to produce. Our problem is that we think in terms of only one fruit: a favorable response. Then we go forth, proclaiming His Word, clutching His promise for fruitfulness, and letting God know in the secret recesses of our hearts that we're counting on Him to deliver up some positive results. But when we fail to see that one fruit that we decided our efforts should produce, we jump to one of three devastating conclusions:

1. We're doing something in the wrong way.

2. God is a liar.

3. God's promise is good for everyone else...but not for me.

The first conclusion—that we're doing something in the wrong way—is very often false. If we haven't violated any of the Lord's commandments in the *doing*, then more often than not, we haven't done anything wrong at all.

The remaining conclusions—that God is a liar, or that God's promise applies to others but not to me—aren't just false; they're heretical.

> **GOD IS ALWAYS USING THE PROCLAMATION OF HIS WORD TO YIELD AT LEAST EIGHT TYPES OF FRUIT.**

We can avoid all of the heartache and hand-wrenching if we acquaint ourselves with what the Scriptures teach us about the full range of fruit that God brings forth whenever we proclaim His good news. He's always using the proclamation of His Word to yield not one, but *at least eight types of fruit*. If we know the fruits, then we should never be crippled by discouragement or doubt. Instead, as the rest of the text in Isaiah 55 tells us, we'll go out with joy, and we'll be led forth with peace—specifically, the peace and confidence of knowing that our labors are never in vain.

What, then, are the fruits that God tells us will always be produced, somewhere, at some point in time, in someone's life? I'll start with the one fruit that we all long to see the most.

THE FRUIT OF SAVING FAITH

Paul categorically states, *"Faith comes from hearing, and hearing by the word of Christ"* (Romans 10:17).

WHAT A REMARKABLE ASSURANCE

Who can begin to number how many lives have come to the Lord because of the Bibles that have been placed in hotel rooms? Who can begin to assess how many souls have been touched—and are being touched every day—by sermons, books, websites, podcasts, songs, tracts, conversations, and every other manner of putting forth the Word of God?

WHAT AN IMMEASURABLE ENCOURAGEMENT

How encouraging it is to know that the birth of faith in someone's life doesn't depend on our intellectual prowess, our character, our acts of kindness, or our ability to persuade. Rather, it rests on the intrinsic power of the living Word. May God forgive us when we take credit for a person's repentance because of what *we* said or did. May God forgive us for condemning ourselves when we conclude that a person's refusal to believe is due to *our* failure to say or do *the right thing*. May we always thank God that the power lies in the ministry of the Holy Spirit and in His inspired message, not in the frail abilities of the messenger. It really makes our "job" so much simpler.

WHAT A CRITICAL REMINDER

God uses His *Word* as the primary agency to create saving faith in a person's life. No wonder, then, that He calls His Word *"the seed"* (Luke 8:11). That seed must be sown because it is the Word that creates life and the fruit of saving faith. The Word must go forth so that people may hear and believe. For how can they believe if they haven't heard, and how can they hear unless the message is proclaimed? (See Romans 10:14.)

But what if we don't see the fruit of saving faith produced in the lives of the people with whom we share that good news? It doesn't matter. Whether we see it or not, the seed will bear fruit somewhere, at some time, in somebody's life. Most of the prophets never saw many people repent. But the message that God's Spirit proclaimed through their lips continues to save lives today.

As for the little old man on 57th Street who sowed the Word of God into my heart back in 1967...I never saw him again. But the words on the scrap of paper that he handed me burrowed deep and blossomed in God's perfect time.

> **SOMETIMES, WE'RE BLESSED WITH UNEXPECTED MOMENTS WHEN WE GET TO SEE THE FRUIT OF SAVING FAITH.**

And then, there are those moments—those unexpected moments—when we do get to see the fruit of saving faith.

One afternoon in the mid-1980s, a sports car screeched to an illegal halt at the curbside as I handed out tracts in West Los Angeles. A moment later, a furious young woman tore out of the driver's side of her car and all but lunged at me, pulling up short no farther than two feet from where I stood. I don't remember anything of what she said because the hostility in her voice drowned out the meaning of her words. After a very long fifteen or thirty seconds, she got back into her car and peeled off.

The verbal attack both startled and stung. But I'd already been berated enough times in the course of ministry to know how to let my feelings go and carry on. Sometime after that, I forgot about the event altogether.

But about three years later, I stood at the back of the auditorium where my colleagues and I held our Friday night messianic worship services. While the worship band played, I noticed a young couple out of the corner of my eye as they entered the hall, not far from where I stood and sang.

"Excuse me," the young woman said politely. I stopped singing and turned in her direction. She looked vaguely familiar, but I couldn't place her face or voice. "This is David," she said, indicating her husband, "and I'm Genevieve. Do you remember me?"

"Not really," I said. "But almost," I added, smiling. "Does that count?

She smiled back, "I nearly trampled you a few years ago in West L.A."

The incident came back. "We didn't get off to a good start, did we?" I asked.

"Actually, we did," she said. "It's just that neither of us knew it at the time." Then she went on to tell me that our first encounter played a major role in her finally coming to faith.

Genevieve, David, and I stayed in fairly close touch from that time on until my wife Ruth and I finally moved to the Soviet Union in 1991. I not only had the joy of meeting Genevieve as a believer, I had the special joy of seeing her flourish as a very gifted evangelist. In light of her ultimate calling, the fierce passion she showed me when we first met made perfect sense.

THE FRUIT OF BIBLICAL DIVISION

The fruit of saving faith is certainly the fruit that we desire to see above all else. But if we measure our effectiveness by the presence of that fruit alone, then we dishonor the power of God's Word. We also destine ourselves for unavoidable disappointment.

Yes, God uses His Word to save. But He also uses His Word to divide. In fact, division is one of the primary fruits of proclamation. That's why Yeshua said, *"I did not come to bring peace, but a sword"* (Matthew 10:34). He's not talking about a physical sword, of course. The sword that He mentions is the sword of taking sides, either for Him or against Him.

Division is biblical and unavoidable because the gospel denies us the option of remaining neutral. Indeed, God warns that if we *"are lukewarm, and neither hot nor cold, I will spit you out of my mouth"* (Revelation 3:16 ESV). Once we've heard and understood, we have to make a choice.

DIVISION IS BIBLICAL AND UNAVOIDABLE BECAUSE THE GOSPEL
DENIES US THE OPTION OF REMAINING NEUTRAL. ONCE WE'VE
HEARD AND UNDERSTOOD, WE HAVE TO MAKE A CHOICE.

We see this polarizing effect of God's Word throughout the entire Scriptures. For example, when Moses brought God's message to Pharaoh, the Lord used His Word to harden his heart. But at the same time, the hearts of some of Pharaoh's servants grew soft. These servants became increasingly convinced that the message Moses delivered needed to be feared, heeded, and obeyed. And so, after Moses issued his warning about the coming destruction of Egypt's livestock, we're told that the servants of Pharaoh who feared the Word of God brought their own servants and livestock safely inside, while others left their livestock and servants outside to die. (See Exodus 9:20–21.)

In short, the Word of God divided Pharaoh's court. And following the tenth plague, on the very day that we Jews left Egypt, Scripture tells us that we didn't depart alone. *"A mixed multitude"* (Exodus 12:38) came out with us. Egyptian society had been divided.

In the same way, the gospel accounts tell us that when Yeshua spoke, some received His message, while others reviled what He had to say. And is there any instance in the Acts of the Apostles when Paul's preaching did not divide the hearers into two groups? Some always rejected the message while others received the Word and believed.

Though it's not a fact that we readily want to admit, scriptural evidence drives us to the conclusion that division is one of the dominant fruits of effective proclamation. We mustn't disparage that truth or disapprove of the way God chooses to work. Whenever the Word of God is openly proclaimed and accurately understood, polarization always occurs. Division is part of its very power.

> *For the word of God is living and active, and sharper than any two-edged sword, even penetrating as far as the division of soul and spirit, of both joints and marrow, and able to judge the thoughts and intentions of the heart.*
>
> (Hebrews 4:12)

Division comes about because the content of the gospel message itself either convicts us of our sin or arouses our self-righteousness. The claim that we're sinful and the call to repent are the stumbling stone and the rock of offense. In light of that offense, we can understand more easily why we're exhorted to share the good news with patience, reverence, and gentleness. The gospel must be communicated in love and with compassion. Why? Because the message itself is so cutting that it hardly needs any additional sharpening from us.

> "CHRIST IN US" WILL DRAW PEOPLE TO HIMSELF. BUT IT WILL ALSO DRIVE SOME PEOPLE AWAY.

But it's not just the declaration of the message that divides. The reality of His Word abiding in us causes division as well. All of us trust that "Christ in us" will draw people to Himself. And He will. But Christ in us—the very presence of Messiah in our lives—will also drive some people away. Paul tells us:

> *For we are a fragrance of Christ to God among those who are being saved and among those who are perishing: to the*

*one an aroma from death to death, to the other an aroma
from life to life.*   (2 Corinthians 2:15–16)

Division—resulting from the Lord's blessing upon our lives
and labors—lies at the heart of the very first conflict between
people that the Bible records. God's approval of Abel's offering
did not inspire Cain to follow the Lord like his brother; instead,
it aroused anger and deadly jealousy. (See Genesis 4:4–8.) The
apostle Paul tells us, *"All who desire to live a godly life in Christ
Jesus will be persecuted"* (2 Timothy 3:12 ESV). And of course,
Jesus Himself told us to expect hostility simply because of our
identification with Him. (See John 15:18–20.)

Living a changed life because of the presence of Messiah in
us will certainly attract some, like a magnet, to the Lord. But a
sanctified life will also repel. Some will be drawn; others will
be driven away. "Christ in us" is by no means a guarantee that
everyone will love us. But it *is* a guarantee that we'll provoke a
response. It is a guarantee that our very lives will divide.

Whether declared with our lips or demonstrated by our
lives and our love, the living Word divides. That's part of its
power. That's one of its fruits.

THE FRUIT OF VINDICATING GOD'S NAME

Yeshua will use our proclamation in the present to prove
He is righteous in the future when He judges the living and the
dead.

We can see this principle in operation in the ministry of the
prophet Ezekiel. Six centuries before the Lord's first coming,
God sent Ezekiel to my ancestors and commanded him to
speak, *"whether they listen or not."* Why? So that *"they will know*

that a prophet has been among them" (Ezekiel 2:5). Ezekiel's ministry made it impossible for us to say that we never had the chance to hear. We were without excuse, as Paul says about all of humanity:

> For since the creation of the world His invisible attributes, that is, His eternal power and divine nature, have been clearly perceived, being understood by what has been made, so that they are **without excuse.**   (Romans 1:20)

In the same way, our proclamation of the gospel today will deny people the opportunity to protest their innocence and plead their ignorance in the future. This is a somber thought.

Perhaps some will stand before Him on that day, hoping that they'll be spared the judgment that disbelief deserves by saying, "I never had the chance to hear."

And if such a scene actually occurs, how might Jesus respond? I can imagine tears filling His eyes as He looks at the ones who insist that they shouldn't be judged. I can imagine Him saying, "*I called and you refused, I stretched out my hand and no one paid attention*" (Proverbs 1:24).

I can imagine the people standing on trial before Him, asking, "When did You call?" And I can imagine Jesus, with a gentle and mournful nod, directing their eyes to some of us, standing quietly nearby.

We were their opportunity to hear.

Our proclamation today will produce the fruit of vindicating God's righteousness in the future, when He judges the living and the dead.

God uses us as people's *"time of...visitation"* (Luke 19:44). Once we're struck by that sobering fact, a radical transformation occurs in the way we react to the scorn we face because of our faith. We still weep. But we don't weep for ourselves; instead, we weep for those who turn us away, even as Jesus wept for the people of Jerusalem. And we still pray. But we don't pray for ourselves; instead, we pray for those who mock and sneer at us, even as Jesus prayed for us from the cross. We weep and we pray for those who reject and revile us because God has used our proclamation to produce another kind of fruit—in *us*...

THE FRUIT OF SHARING YESHUA'S COMPASSION FOR THE LOST

This is not a natural fruit. It's cultivated by God, and more often than not, it rises out of the soil of rejection after the gospel seed has been sown. Moses possessed that fruit. After we'd spurned God's goodness by worshipping a golden calf, he pleaded with God on our behalf. Though our idolatry was as much a rejection of Moses as it was a rejection of the Lord, Moses implored God for our sake.

> But now, if You will forgive their sin, very well; but if not, please wipe me out from Your book which You have written!   (Exodus 32:32)

The disciple Stephen possessed that heart of compassion as well. Moments before succumbing to his death by stoning, he cried, *"Lord, do not hold this sin against them!"* (Acts 7:60).

God produces some measure of that fruit in our own lives as we carry His message to others.

In the 1980s, I had the privilege of leading a man named Rafi to the Lord. For the first few weeks after his profession of faith, his joy and excitement grew as his relationship with Yeshua seemed to deepen every day. We'd meet to read the Scriptures and pray. And at almost every meeting, he'd tell me some new story about how the Lord had answered a specific prayer.

Then it all changed.

The meetings became fewer and fewer; there always seemed to be a reason for Rafi to cancel or postpone them. And when we did meet, he no longer talked of new insights or answered prayers. Instead, he raised questions that sounded more like poorly concealed objections rather than genuine requests for deeper understanding. From a few of his unguarded and caustic remarks, I pieced together what had taken place.

Rafi met regularly on weekends with other Israelis for an impromptu game of football (soccer) at a local park. When he told them about his new faith, he encountered disinterest, then disdain, and finally scorn.

I knew that I needed to urge Rafi to stand firm, to suffer the rejection, and to count it all joy for the privilege of being identified with the One who was despised and not esteemed. (See Isaiah 53:3.) So, I called and asked him if I could stop by. Rafi agreed, reluctantly.

When I arrived at his apartment, he opened the door and then stepped back. He said nothing. He simply let me in. He never sat down, and he never invited me to sit. He just observed me while I spoke.

When I finished, he said in a colorless tone, "Is that it?"

"Yes," I said softly, "that's it."

"Well, okay then," he said. He walked back to the door and opened it again, letting me know that it was time for me to leave.

"We'll talk again soon," I said, more as an offer than a promise.

"Take care," he said flatly.

> **SOMETIMES WHEN WE EVANGELIZE AND THE GOOD NEWS IS REJECTED, GOD ALLOWS US TO FEEL HIS SORROW.**

As I drove away, I prayed that the Lord would turn Rafi around and grant him a renewed, deepened faith. I prayed with a burdened heart because Rafi's rejection hurt. But oddly enough, I felt no personal pain from his rejection. My sorrow stemmed from my understanding that Rafi had rejected the Lord. In His grace, God had used this tragic episode to nurture in my own heart something of the sorrow that *He* felt over Rafi's choice. God granted me the privilege of tasting a portion of His compassion for the lost. That God-given compassion is fruit. It comes from proclaiming the good news.

THE FRUIT OF INCREASED SIN, INCREASED ACCOUNTABILITY, AND ABOUNDING GRACE

Scripture candidly and uncomfortably recounts many times when the proclamation of God's message by His prophets brought about the progressive hardening of the people's hearts, and therefore, an increase in their sin. The outworking of this process helps us understand what Yeshua meant when He said, *"If I had not come and spoken to them, they would not have sin; but now they have no excuse for their sin"* (John 15:22).

Isaiah also makes it clear that the Lord intended to use the prophet's proclamation for the purpose of bringing about a greater turning away. On the very day that Isaiah received his call, the Lord explained that his proclamation would actually harden people's hearts, deafen their ears, and make their eyes dim with disbelief. (See Isaiah 6:9–10.)

It is a startling and distressing spiritual truth—the presentation of the Word increases sin. But does the reality of that truth make God Himself unkind or, even worse, unjust? Would it have been better if He'd never spoken to us through the Law, the Prophets, and ultimately through the Son? Not at all. For when the Word confronts us with our sin, we're also confronted with the challenge and opportunity to repent. When God confronted Cain with the evil in his heart, He warned him of the ultimate outcome, and He implored him to turn around. (See Genesis 4:6–7.)

> **WHEN THE WORD CONFRONTS US WITH OUR SIN, WE'RE ALSO CONFRONTED WITH THE CHALLENGE AND OPPORTUNITY TO REPENT.**

It would be tragic indeed if the matter ended with the progressive hardening of our hearts. But whenever we seize the opportunity that God affords us to repent, then His greater grace proves to be the antidote to our increased sin. This is why Paul could explain, "*The Law came in so that the offense would increase; but where sin increased, grace abounded all the more*" (Romans 5:20).

Greater sin, greater accountability, and greater grace, all abounding to the greater glory of God, are fruit of the proclamation of His Word.

THE FRUIT OF CLEAN HANDS AND CLEAR CONSCIENCES

When Paul argued for the gospel in the synagogue at Corinth, he received mixed reactions from his listeners. (See Acts 18:4–8.) We're told that a number of Greeks and some Jewish people believed, including Crispus, the leader of the synagogue. But we're also told that others in the congregation resisted and even blasphemed the name of the Lord. In response to that opposition, Paul uttered words that on the surface might sound like an imprecation: *"Your blood is on your own heads! I am clean"* (verse 6). Did he indeed utter a curse? No, he voiced a principle. In fact, he paraphrased an important warning that the Lord gave to Ezekiel:

> *When I say to the wicked, "You wicked person, you will certainly die," and you do not speak to warn the wicked about his way, that wicked person shall die for his wrongdoing, but I will require his blood from your hand. But if you on your part warn a wicked person to turn from his way and he does not turn from his way, he will die for his wrongdoing, but you have saved your life.* (Ezekiel 33:8–9)

It's a disconcerting thought, but we need to take it to heart all the same. We will be held accountable for our silence. When we fail to speak as we should, the blood of the *"wicked person"* in some way covers our hands. But the proclamation of the gospel keeps our hands clean, even as Paul said when he brought the good news to Corinth. Clean hands and clear consciences are fruit of the proclamation of the gospel—fruit that blossoms to the benefit of the one who proclaims the Word of God.

THE FRUIT OF CONFORMITY TO HIS IMAGE

Theologically speaking, we know that Yeshua really doesn't *need* us to do anything to bring people to Himself. If He wanted, He could merely speak the Word, and the task of world evangelization would be finished. But throughout history, He's always chosen to use sinful, imperfect people to accomplish His holy and perfect plans. Why? Let me tell you a story that has helped me to understand a little bit of the mystery.

More than thirty years ago, I had decided to paint a room in our home, but I wasn't looking forward to the task, by any means. As I stared at the walls and the paint in anything but a good frame of mind, my four-year-old son Joel wandered into the room.

"What are you doing?" he asked.

"Painting the room," I replied flatly.

Joel's eyes grew very wide. "Can I help?!"

Every bone in my body—in fact, every fiber of my being—silently cried out, *No!* That's the normal response of a man trying to get the job done in the most efficient manner possible. Otherwise, the task would take at least twice as long. I'd have to "fix" all of my young son's work by repainting everything he painted and then spend a good deal of time cleaning up all the paint he would undoubtedly splatter about. The logical, sensible answer to his request to let him help would be, "That's all right,

Joel. You just sit over there and watch. I'll paint the room by myself."

But by God's grace, and to my own surprise, I heard myself say, "Sure, Joel. You can help."

And so, for the next few hours, we painted the room together—which means that, just as I thought, the task took twice as long as it should have taken. And after he left to take a nap, I set about repainting everything he'd painted and cleaning up all the places where he'd splattered the paint.

> **JESUS INVITES US TO FELLOWSHIP WITH HIM AND IMITATE HIM SO THAT WE BECOME MORE LIKE HIM.**

So why did I say yes to his request? The parental instinct in me told me that more than the mere painting of a room was at stake. By telling him, "Yes, you can help," I invited him to fellowship with me and to imitate me. And he did.

He watched me closely. He listened to my instructions. He tried to paint the way I painted. In a word, he committed himself to the task of being just like me. The experience deepened our relationship and filled him with joy.

One of the most endearing memories I harbor from my son's early years occurred on that day. At one point, my wife Ruth walked into the room, looked at the disorder masquerading as a paint job, and asked, "What are you two doing?"

Joel answered with uncensored pride, "*We're* painting the room."

Paul told the Corinthians, *"Be imitators of me, just as I also am of Christ"* (1 Corinthians 11:1). When we proclaim the gospel, we are doing what He did for most of the three years that He spent ministering among us on earth. But in order to do that, we need to watch Him closely. We need to listen to His instructions. And as we do what He did, His Holy Spirit makes us more like Him. We learn humility. We learn to depend upon His grace. We learn to obey. We learn to deny ourselves, pick up our cross, and follow. As we learn, we're conformed more and more into His image by the power of His Spirit through the renewing of our minds.

When we proclaim the gospel, He makes us more like Him.

THE FRUIT OF JOY AND PEACE

God produces at least one more type of fruit whenever we proclaim His good news—the fruit of joy and peace. (See Isaiah 55:12.)

We read in the book of Hebrews that the Lord endured the cross and disdained the shame because of the joy set before Him. (See Hebrews 12:2.) What joy? The joy of knowing that multitudes would be reconciled to the Father throughout the centuries because of His act of obedience.

We are that very joy that He envisioned. In His perfect humanity, Yeshua agonized under the weight of the physical and emotional torment that accompanied His crucifixion. But in His perfect deity, He rejoiced over the names and faces of each individual whom He foreknew and predestined to come to Him. He rejoiced specifically over each one of *us*.

You and I can't know the names or see the faces of every life that will be touched by our proclamation. But we can possess that very joy that Jesus possessed. It's the joy and peace that comes from knowing with unshakable confidence that our labors today will produce an eternal impact on people whom we may not even meet until we're together with them after Yeshua has returned.

ABUNDANT, ABIDING FRUIT

The proclamation of the Word always produces fruit. Always. The fruit of saving faith. The fruit of biblical division. The fruit of vindicating His righteousness while increasing our compassion for the lost. The fruit of progressive sin, increased accountability, and greater grace, all abounding to the glory of His name. The fruit of keeping our hands clean and our consciences clear. The fruit of being conformed into the image of His Son. The fruit of joy and peace.

We need to guard our hearts against any ungodly discouragement that may arise from an ignorance of how God works through the proclamation of His good news. Perhaps more importantly, we need to guard our hearts from the sin of ingratitude when, like selfish children who didn't get their way, we scold God in our hearts because He didn't produce the fruit that *we* want to see.

> **PROCLAIMING THE GOSPEL ALWAYS PRODUCES FRUIT, NO MATTER WHO IS DELIVERING THE MESSAGE.**

One of the most astonishing guarantees about the fruitfulness of proclaiming the gospel is found in the book of Philippians. Writing while imprisoned in Rome, Paul described the mixed bag of motives driving different people to preach the gospel during his confinement. He admitted that while some declared the message out of a love for Paul and the gospel that he had delivered to them, others proclaimed the message *"out of selfish ambition...thinking that they are causing me distress"* (Philippians 1:17).

And then, amazingly, Paul essentially went on to say, "So what!" For *"in every way, whether in pretense or in truth, Christ is proclaimed, and in this I rejoice"* (verse 18).

Paul rejoiced because he knew that, regardless of the motive, the proclamation of the message would bear fruit because the power doesn't rest with the messenger. It rests in the message. Does that guarantee then grant us the liberty to proclaim the gospel from base motives and desires? Does it release us from the responsibility to speak the truth in love, deference, and respect? No, it doesn't. May the meditations of our hearts and the words of our lips always honor the Lord! But whether our hearts and lips are sullied or pure, the proclamation of the gospel produces fruit because the message of Jesus alone remains the power of God.

There's only one way for the Word to become unfruitful—and that's if it's never proclaimed. No wonder Paul wrote, *"Be steadfast, immovable, always abounding in the work of the Lord, knowing that in the Lord your labor is not in vain"* (1 Corinthians 15:58 ESV).

From time to time, I think of the little old man I met on 57th Street back in 1967. I'm grateful for that encounter, but I have one regret: I can't picture his face. To be honest, I'm not even certain if I ever bothered to glance at his face. I only remember that he looked old and uncomfortable, yet he was determined to hand out his scraps of paper. More than that, I really can't recall.

But after Jesus comes back, I'll know who that little old man is. So, I've decided that I'll walk up to him someday after the Lord's return. I'll approach him from behind, and I'll tap him on the shoulder. When he turns around, I'll look into his face, and I'll say, "In 1967, you gave me a piece of paper with the words of John 3:16 written on it. The Lord used that piece of paper to start changing my life."

I suspect he'll answer with a grin and a matter-of-fact shrug. I imagine he'll say, "I know. I've read Isaiah 55."

THREE

THE FEARS THAT SHUT OUR MOUTHS

If we know that the proclamation of His Word always brings forth abundant fruit, why do we find it so hard to sow the seed?

I knew a missionary in Ukraine who had a reputation among his colleagues for being genuinely courageous. He was no stranger to physical violence or verbal attacks, but neither seemed to stop him. I asked him once if he came by his courage naturally, and he shook his head no. "So, how do you account for it?" I asked.

"Truthfully?" he asked back.

"Truthfully," I replied.

"Twice in my life, I ran away. The taste was so bitter, I prayed that I'd never taste it again."

What struck me wasn't the source of his courage, but the admission of his cowardice.

Let me take you to a pivotal moment in the history of the world. It's the watershed event in which the apostle Paul struggled so intensely with fear that he ran the risk of choosing silence instead of continuing to proclaim the good news. It's the breaking point when he confronted and overcame his fear, when he decided not to be frightened and not to be silent, but to speak.

Paul arrived in the Greek city of Corinth sometime after 49 BC, following a lukewarm reaction to his ministry in Athens. He longed to get to Rome, but a recent decree from the emperor Claudius had banished us Jews from the imperial capital, and Corinth became one of the focal points for Jewish refugees. Among them were a husband and wife named Aquila and Priscilla, who befriended the apostle. Like Paul, they believed in Yeshua, and like Paul, they made tents for a living. That tent-making business provided a livelihood so that Paul could go about doing what he'd come to Corinth to do: openly proclaim the good news.

And Paul was reasoning in the synagogue every Sabbath and trying to persuade Jews and Greeks.   (Acts 18:4)

PAUL'S IMPACT ON CORINTH

Paul's "reasoning" paid off. The fact that he presented the gospel message "every Sabbath" tells us clearly that there were those who wanted to hear what he had to say. But whenever there's interest, opposition isn't far away. When his opponents crossed the line from disbelief to blasphemy, Paul halted his work in that particular synagogue and moved his evangelistic activities next door—far enough away to be outside of the synagogue, but close enough to be a constant reminder to the people that they had to make a choice. And while some resisted and blasphemed, others believed. In fact, *"Crispus, the leader of the synagogue, believed in the Lord together with his entire household; and many of the Corinthians, as they listened to Paul, were believing and being baptized"* (verse 8).

So much for Paul's impact on Corinth. But what about…

CORINTH'S IMPACT ON PAUL

He was terrified.

We don't generally think of Paul as a man who wrestled with fear. We know that the other apostles had to wage that inner battle. On the night of Yeshua's arrest, every apostle except for John deserted Him. Even Peter, the boorish Galilean who declared that he'd never abandon the Lord, ended up denying Him three times after His arrest. (See John 18:15–27.) From the divine perspective, the denial fulfilled Yeshua's prophetic word. (See Luke 22:34, 61.) From a human perspective, the betrayal revealed Peter's naked fear.

Nor did the apostles' fears suddenly evaporate into a mist after Yeshua's resurrection. Though they possessed the evidence of the empty tomb and heard the clear and emphatic testimony from Mary Magdalene that Jesus had been raised from the dead, the apostles still cowered behind bolted doors out of fear for their lives. (See John 20:19.)

When we think of Paul, however, "fear" hardly fits our image of the committed, dauntless provocateur. But cherished images notwithstanding, Paul struggled with fear. So much so, in fact, that the Lord Himself had to appear to Paul in Corinth, in a nighttime vision, and give him a stern rebuke. *"Do not be afraid any longer, but go on speaking and do not be silent"* (Acts 18:9).

> **DESPITE A FRUITFUL MINISTRY, PAUL WAS GRIPPED BY FEAR SO FORCEFULLY THAT HE WAS APPARENTLY TEMPTED TO STOP SPREADING THE GOSPEL.**

Was he really afraid? Isn't it possible that the Lord just appeared as a preventative measure? No, Paul was terrified. Years later, Paul wrote back to the Corinthians and reminded them, *"I also was with you in weakness and fear, and in great trembling"* (1 Corinthians 2:3). Despite a fruitful ministry, Paul was gripped by fear so forcefully that he was apparently tempted to stop speaking out.

FIVE FEARS THAT SHUT OUR MOUTHS

What accounted for this fear? We can take a healthy guess, based on what the Lord said to Paul. *"I am with you, and no one will attack you to harm you, for I have many people in this city"* (Acts 18:10). The words suggest that Paul feared three things: abandonment, physical harm, and fruitless labors.

Paul's experience is not unique; these three terrors, along with two others, make up a list of fears that commonly cause us to muzzle ourselves when it comes to proclaiming the gospel message. The other two fears that stifle our voices are the fear of incompetence or "doing it wrong," and the fear of rejection.

I've found no evidence in Scripture to suggest that Paul ever struggled with these other two fears, but the rest of us certainly know them well enough as relentless adversaries. Taken all together, these five are the fears that shut our mouths. Let me look at each fear in turn, starting with the ones that crippled the apostle Paul.

FEAR OF ABANDONMENT

Many times throughout Scripture, the Lord reassures us: "*I am with you.*" Yet the fear of abandonment underscores so much of my people's biblical history. Our distrust of God caused us to conclude that He would *not* be with us if we were to cross the Jordan, attack the walled cities of Canaan, and take on the giant Anakim. (See Deuteronomy 1:26–33.) Tragically, our fear of abandonment and our unbelief caused the exodus generation to forfeit the land.

Moses knew this fear of abandonment as well, and he cried to the Lord, "*If Your presence does not go with us, do not lead us up from here*" (Exodus 33:15). And how often did David plead, "*Do not abandon me nor forsake me, God of my salvation!*" (Psalm 27:9; see also Psalms 38:21; 71:9, 18; 138:8). It's little wonder, then, that the Lord assured Paul with the same words that He consistently used to assure His people in the Law and the Prophets: "*Do not fear, for I am with you*" (Genesis 26:24; see also Isaiah 41:10; 43:5; Jeremiah 42:11; 46:28).

GOD HAS ALWAYS BOLSTERED OUR FRAGILE RESOLVE WITH THE GUARANTEE OF HIS UNFAILING PRESENCE.

In His extravagant grace and compassion toward us, His halting servants, God has always bolstered our fragile resolve with the guarantee of His unfailing presence. God understood Moses's anxieties about returning to Egypt in order to confront Pharaoh, and so He assured the reluctant redeemer, "*Assuredly I will be with you*" (Exodus 3:12). A generation later, He allayed Joshua's fears by promising, "*Just as I have been with Moses, I will be with you*" (Joshua 1:5). And even though David often begged God not to abandon him, he knew on the basis of God's unbreakable faithfulness that he would not be forsaken, and that he needn't fear. "*Even though I walk through the valley of the shadow of death, I fear no evil, for You are with me*" (Psalm 23:4).

Not surprisingly, then, just before His ascension, the Lord promised His disciples, "*I am with you always, to the end of the age*" (Matthew 28:20).

God's unwavering pledge to be with us is not just a statement of His geography; it's a statement of His identity as well. His very name, Emanuel, means "God is with us." (See Isaiah 7:14.) He cannot be the covenantal God of Abraham, Isaac, and Jacob without being the God who will never leave us or forsake us. "*I am with you*" is His very being. Abandonment simply isn't an option, and so, we needn't fear.

FEAR OF PHYSICAL HARM

And what about Paul's fear of being harmed?

The apostle was well acquainted with physical violence, both at the hands of us, his fellow Jews, as well as from gentiles. Even before his arrival in Corinth, Paul had already been beaten, flogged, and stoned in the course of his missionary work. But in every instance, the Lord protected and delivered

Paul. Nevertheless, despite God's unbroken track record of deliverance, Paul wrestled with a fear of physical harm. Coming to Paul in a vision at night, Jesus said, *"No one will attack you to harm you"* (Acts 18:10).

Not long afterward, Paul came to realize a cardinal spiritual truth: nothing could really harm him, even if he were to be mauled or put to death. That's why he later wrote:

> *For I am convinced that neither death, nor life, nor angels, nor principalities, nor things present, nor things to come, nor powers, nor height, nor depth, nor any other created thing will be able to separate us from the love of God that is in Christ Jesus our Lord.*   (Romans 8:38–39)

Paul understood that he stood indestructible before people because he remained inseparable from Christ. And so, he explained to the Philippians, *"For to me, to live is Christ, and to die is gain"* (Philippians 1:21).

What could have given Paul that empowering insight? Certainly, the *usefulness* of the harm that he endured. Later, he explained to the Corinthians, *"Our momentary, light affliction is producing for us an eternal weight of glory far beyond all comparison"* (2 Corinthians 4:17). Paul knew that all things, even his sufferings, worked together for good to those who loved the Lord and were called to accomplish His purposes. (See Romans 8:28.)

> **ALL THINGS WORK TOGETHER FOR GOOD WHEN WE LOVE THE LORD AND STRIVE TO ACCOMPLISH HIS PURPOSES.**

What else could have given Paul the understanding that whether he lived or died, he faced a *no lose* situation? Undoubtedly, the relative insignificance of his current sufferings compared to the glory that lay ahead. (See Romans 8:18.)

And perhaps the horrifying end confronting the lost helped Paul keep his own hardships in proper perspective. This perspective caused him to confess with a broken, agonizing heart, *"I could wish that I myself were accursed, separated from Christ for the sake of my countrymen, my kinsmen according to the flesh, who are Israelites"* (Romans 9:3–4). Remembering the greater plight of others is always a good antidote to obsessing over our own hardships.

If Something Happens, It's No Big Deal

I had a colleague from the UK named Lawrence who joined our London team for a season. One afternoon, we readied ourselves for a street outreach that ran no risk of being anything other than normal. Lawrence sat off to the side, clearly worried and apprehensive. So I sat down next to him and said, "Nothing will happen. And even if it does, it won't be any big deal."

"You know this?" he challenged.

"I know this," I answered.

"Truth be told," Lawrence said with proper British reserve, "I don't think I can do this."

I decided to change the subject—but not really—by asking him what he studied at university.

"Economics," Lawrence said.

"I'm impressed," I said with a smile. "Did you ever play any sports?"

"I did," he said, absently.

"What did you play?"

"Just some football"—that is, soccer.

"Football. Quite a sport. Pretty physical. I never played."

Lawrence said nothing, and I suspect he would have been happy to let the conversation end. But I went on.

"Tell me, before heading out onto the pitch, did you ever wrestle with the fear of getting hurt?"

"That was different," Lawrence quickly joined back in, soft but insistent.

"How so?"

"No one was deliberately trying to hurt me."

I unpacked his reasoning further. "So, if something *did* happen, you knew it wasn't personal. Just part of what happens sometimes. Then you probably got up, shook it off, and carried on. Am I right?"

"That was different," he repeated more emphatically than before.

"No," I countered quietly. "It's not."

Nothing out of the ordinary happened during that afternoon outreach, and Lawrence did just fine.

Paul understood that even if attacked, tortured, or killed, nothing could harm him. We should have that same understanding.

FEAR OF FAILURE OR FRUITLESS LABORS

Did Paul fear failure or fruitless endeavor? Apparently, he did. We get a glimpse of his anxiety over the prospect of having squandered his time and efforts when we read his letter to the Galatians. Scolding them for being foolish (see Galatians 3:1), he anxiously wonders, *"Perhaps I have labored over you in vain"* (Galatian 4:11).

It's clear from both the passage in Acts 18 as well as from Paul's letter to the Galatians that there were definite times in Paul's life when he feared that his efforts at preaching the gospel would fail to bear fruit. So, the Lord assured him in Corinth, *"I have many people in this city"* (Acts 18:10). These were people to reach for the Lord and people to teach the Lord's ways.

Ultimately, any fears of failure that might have plagued Paul's heart and mind were laid to rest by the time he wrote back to the Corinthians years later. In his first letter to them, he urged them to press on, *"always excelling in the work of the Lord, knowing that your labor is not in vain in the Lord"* (1 Corinthians 15:58).

And as he neared the end of his life, Paul wrote with absolute confidence that his own labors had not amounted to a waste of time and effort. *"I am convinced that He is able to protect what I have entrusted to Him until that day"* (2 Timothy 1:12). Paul's confidence didn't rest in visible results, but in his certainty about the trustworthiness of God.

NOTHING WE DO IN FAITH AND OBEDIENCE TO GOD IS EVER IN VAIN.

Nothing we do in faith and obedience to God is ever in vain, whether we conquer kingdoms and shut the mouths of lions, or whether we experience mocking, scourging, or being sawn in two. (See Hebrews 11:32–37.)

We cannot lose. Our labor in the Lord is never in vain.

So much for Paul's fears. But what about the other two monsters in the closet that didn't seem to plague the apostle, but which gnaw at our faith and keep us up at night? What about the fear of incompetence and the fear of rejection?

FEAR OF INCOMPETENCE

When the Lord told Moses that He was sending him back to Egypt in order to redeem us from our bondage to Pharaoh, the murderer-turned-shepherd recoiled.

> *Who am I, that I should go to Pharaoh, and that I should bring the sons of Israel out of Egypt?...Now they may say to me, "What is His name?" What shall I say to them?*
> (Exodus 3:11, 13)

Moses felt he had a credibility problem. In truth, he did... and he didn't. Moses didn't have any credibility or competence of his own, but God didn't require him to be credible or competent. God required him to be confident in God's power and obedient to God's instructions. God responded to Moses's fear of incompetence with a threefold assurance. He promised Moses His presence, His delegated authority, and the demonstration of His miraculous power. (See Exodus 3:12, 14, 20.) But we shouldn't miss the subtle irony. At no time did the Lord tell Moses, "Don't belittle yourself. You *are* up to the task." In essence, He told him, "*I the Lord* am up to the task." God's assurances had nothing to do with Moses; they had everything to do with God.

The fact of the matter is, Moses *was* incompetent, and so are we. But God doesn't call us to be competent. He calls us to be available (see Isaiah 6:8), prepared (see 2 Timothy 2:15), and truthful (see Proverbs 14:25). In fact, He delights in using the incompetent, the base, and the inglorious in order to guarantee that the glory goes exclusively to Him.

God's Unique Champions

Have you ever noticed the counterintuitive pattern that seems to characterize so many of God's choices when it comes to selecting His *champions?*

+ He chose Abraham, an old man *"as good as dead"* (Romans 4:19), and his wife Sarah, who was beyond her childbearing years, to be the progenitors of His chosen people. (See Genesis 12:1–3.)

+ He used Moses, an aged, outlawed shepherd with a speech impediment, to humble the mightiest man on earth. (See Exodus 3:10.)

+ He used Rahab, a prostitute, to protect Joshua's scouts and to share in the line of descent that led to the Savior of the world. (See Joshua 2:1–21; Matthew 1:5.)

+ He used David, a boy with a sling, to defeat the giant of Gath. (See 1 Samuel 17:50.)

+ He used a vacillating Gideon and three hundred men who drank water like dogs to route a Midianite army whose numbers were like the sands of the shore. (See Judges 7:7; 8:10.)

+ He used Peter, a brutish fisherman from the ignoble *"Galilee of the Gentiles"* (Isaiah 9:1) to confront the religious elite with the message of the cross. (See Acts 4:1–22.)

+ And He used Rabbi Saul of Tarsus, an irascible, frail, and (according to tradition) ugly little man to bring the gospel to a Greco-Roman world that idolized beauty, refinement, and strength. (See Acts 9:15.)

God doesn't call us to be competent, although He does prepare and equip us for the tasks He commissions us to perform. He grants us the appropriate gifts of His Spirit, and He places us in the cauldron of experience, not just for our sanctification, but for our growth as effective workers. But our effectiveness doesn't rest in our expertise. From God's side of the equation, our effectiveness rests in His grace. From our side of the equation, our effectiveness rests in our faithful obedience, in our adherence to *His best practices*, and, first and foremost, in our faith and confidence in Him.

> **GOD NEVER MAKES US FULLY UP TO THE TASK HE HAS FOR US BECAUSE HE WANTS US TO RELY ON HIM.**

And even though He prepares us beforehand for what He calls us to do, He never makes us fully up to the task. We always find ourselves at least a little bit in water that's over our heads. He wants us relying on His sufficiency, not our own. The balance between our inadequacy and God's omnipotence, between our weakness and His limitless might, is best summarized by Paul: *"When I am weak, then I am strong"* (2 Corinthians 12:10). *"I can do all things through Him who strengthens me"* (Philippians 4:13).

My father's definition of an *authority* was anyone who travels more than fifty kilometers to give an opinion. The Lord may call us to travel, but He hasn't called us to be authorities or experts. He's summoned us to be His *witnesses*. In a court of law, witnesses really have a very simple and narrow task. They're required to state what they know to be true.

Do we have to be experts? I suppose it couldn't hurt. But what kind of experts did the Lord include in His entourage when He walked among us on earth? Fishermen, tax collectors, reformed prostitutes, cleansed lepers, and demoniacs restored to mental health, to name a few. What made them competent was their commitment to state the truth. *"What we have heard, what we have seen with our eyes, what we have looked at and touched with our hands, concerning the Word of Life…we proclaim to you"* (1 John 1:1, 3).

Our competence resides in and with God. Our credibility rests in our commitment to speak the truth.

But isn't there a danger and a likelihood that we'll make mistakes as we witness for the Lord? Actually, there's more— there's a guarantee that we'll blunder. Sad to say, we'll never lack those times when we fail to seize the right moment, or speak the proper words, or walk away from an inappropriate exchange. But can we sabotage God's plans? No, we can't. As overly simplistic as it may sound, we cannot turn off whomever the Holy Spirit is turning on. God never surrenders control.

Granted, we mustn't presume upon God's grace and use His sovereign control as an excuse for poor preparation or sloppy labor. But at the same time, we mustn't cripple ourselves by fearing that our mistakes can invalidate God's plans. There's both a sobering reminder and a comforting assurance in that thought. The reminder is this: ultimately, no one receives God's gift of eternal life because of how brilliantly we witnessed, or how lovingly we behaved. And what's the assurance? Just this: no one perishes because of how stupidly we spoke or performed.

We needn't fear doing it wrong because, in a sense, we never really do it *right*. If He wanted it all done right without any mistakes, then He'd just do it all Himself. But God doesn't do that. Instead, He calls us to act, and He fixes our mistakes, all the while delighting in our obedience and trust.

FEAR OF REJECTION

Moses admitted to at least one more fear—the fear of rejection. He asked the Lord, *"What if they will not believe me?"* (Exodus 4:1). In comfortable, affluent, and tolerant societies where the greatest cost of discipleship might be the sacrifice of relationships and the loss of status or prestige, this is the fear that cripples us the most. When Moses voiced his fear of rejection in Exodus 3–4, the Lord's assurance amounted to a blunt assessment of the responses that Moses could expect to face. Some would listen (see Exodus 3:18), and some would not (see Exodus 7:4). Either way, God commanded him to speak.

God placed the same challenge before Ezekiel, eight hundred years later. God told the prophet to speak, *"whether they listen or not"* (Ezekiel 2:5). God places the same challenge before us today.

> ALL TOO OFTEN, WE FEAR THE REJECTION OF PEOPLE MORE THAN WE FEAR GOD'S DISPLEASURE.

We need to confront some unpleasant truths about our fear of rejection. All too often, we fear the rejection of people more than we fear invoking the displeasure of God. But rather than admit our greater fear of people, we conceal it with self-flattering words. "Well, I don't want to offend anyone," we tell ourselves with dishonest humility. A more truthful self-assessment would be, "I don't want people to dislike me. I don't want to be cut off from them."

Our fear of rejection actually goes much further back than we think—all the way back to the garden of Eden. We fear rejection because we *are* rejected. When Adam and Eve disobeyed the Lord, they died spiritually and were cast out of His presence. Rejected. We inherit that spiritual death, and we sense that rejection on some primal and subliminal plane. The tragic irony is that we spend our lives seeking acceptance from *people* rather than seeking acceptance from the Lord. We need to cultivate a proper perspective on the matter: What people think of us is not important. The only thing that matters is what the *Lord* thinks of us.

Decades ago, Moishe Rosen, the founder of the ministry Jews for Jesus, told many of us, his younger colleagues, "We believers have got it backwards. We're supposed to have faces of flint and hearts of flesh. But we don't. We have faces of flesh, and hearts of flint. The slightest nasty look sends us running. Shame on us."

It's a disgraceful paradox. On the one hand, the same all-powerful Spirit of God who raised the man Jesus from the dead now lives and works in us. And yet, on the other hand, we're immobilized by a fear of suffering some imaginary, irreparable emotional scarring if someone so much as looks at us with the slightest hint of disapproval or disdain. Moishe had it right; shame on us.

So how can we develop faces of flint and hearts of flesh?

Here's the first step: let's understand the *irrelevance* of our fear of rejection. Our rejection *is* relevant only if it's due to wrongdoing on our part. And in that case, we must repent and seek forgiveness. But if we suffer rejection for speaking the truth in love, then our rejection isn't relevant at all. Just as the Lord told Ezekiel, we must spread the gospel whether people listen or not. *"And whoever does not receive you nor listen to your words… shake the dust off your feet"* (Matthew 10:14). That's not an invitation for us to be callous or uncaring toward those who reject us. But it *is* an admonition to be unscathed and undeterred by the rejection itself.

WHEN THE GOOD NEWS IS SPURNED, PEOPLE ARE REJECTING GOD, NOT US.

Let's accept the fact that rejection by some is an unavoidable given. May our hearts always break when the good news is spurned, but not because people are rejecting *us*. Rather, may our hearts anguish over the fact that people are rejecting *Him*. This leads me to my next point.

We should keep in mind who's being rejected. God told Samuel—and He tells us as well—*"They have not rejected you, but they have rejected Me"* (1 Samuel 8:7). This sobering truth should compel us to worry less about ourselves and more about the ones who are making such a fatal mistake. Like Samuel, our response to people's rejection of the Lord should be the earnest pledge to plead for them in prayer.

At the same time, let us embrace the honor of the rejection we face, because it originates in our identification with the Lord. What a privilege. Yeshua told us, *"A slave is not greater than his master"* (John 15:20). Just as Jesus endured persecution, we must expect to be persecuted as well.

Finally, let us not mourn over our rejection by people. Rather, let us give thanks and rejoice over our acceptance by God. Even when men and women call us cursed, He calls us His beloved. (See Romans 1:7.)

DANGER AWAITS *US* IF WE'RE SILENT

There are dangers to our ministries and our very lives if we choose to tolerate and justify the fears that shut our mouths.

There is the danger of deliberate disobedience. Choosing silence out of fear is functionally the same as being ashamed of the Lord. And we know how Jesus feels about that. (See Mark 8:38.)

Then, there is the danger of cultivating a chronic fear that never quits. A fear that shuts our mouths can become a habit that silences us all our lives.

A bit more subtle is the danger of delaying or becoming indecisive when we clearly know that God wants us to act. We tell ourselves that we have to know more before we can speak out on behalf of the Lord. Or, we tell ourselves that we have to build a platform of friendship before a person will listen to what we have to say. Friendships are good, and platforms are helpful, but not essential. If we've ever been impacted by a book, a song, a recording, or a message from a person we've never met, then we know that a platform of friendship is not a mandatory prerequisite—not unless the author first spent months befriending you before cautiously inviting you to read his or her book.

The danger of diversion is the close cousin of the type of delay I've just described above. We become methodological perfectionists, which means that we end up doing nothing. We spend not some but all of our time searching for the right method rather than trusting that the *message* will do its work.

Another danger is displacement, which lures us into changing or replacing the message of the cross with something more popular, more acceptable—in short, more marketable—and quite often false.

> **WHETHER WE'RE GIFTED OR NOT,**
> **WE'RE EXPECTED TO EXERCISE BASIC SPIRITUAL DISCIPLINES—**
> **INCLUDING SPREADING THE GOSPEL.**

The danger of deferring convinces us that we don't need to speak because "I'm not called to evangelize; that's not my gift. God will use others to speak." To be frank, we could apply the same rationale toward any spiritual discipline that we don't especially care to practice. We could say, "I'm not called to pray; I'm not called to read the Bible; I'm not called to fellowship with others; I'm not called to give. That's not my gifting." It's certainly true that the Lord gives certain people the gift of evangelism, but whether we're gifted or not, we're expected to exercise basic spiritual disciplines like praying, reading His Word, fellowshipping, giving, and telling others what we believe. When Peter wrote to believers in the dispersion to be ready at all times to give an account for the *hope* we possess, he didn't write exclusively to evangelists; he wrote to the body at large:

*Sanctify Christ as Lord in your hearts, **always being ready
to make a defense to everyone who asks you to give an
account for the hope that is in you**, but with gentleness
and respect.*   (1 Peter 3:15)

As for God using someone else, I smile whenever I read
about the moment when the Lord asked Isaiah, *"Whom shall I
send, and who will go for Us?"* (Isaiah 6:8). I smile because when
God asked the question, there was no one else in the room.

Finally, the more we shut our mouths out of fear, the more
we flirt with the danger of eroding our personal faith. We have
to justify our silence somehow, after all. So we conclude that we
really don't need to speak because some people really don't need
to hear. Soon, whether we admit it or not, we convince ourselves
that no one really needs to hear, including us.

But as strong as the fears that shut our mouths might seem
to be, the assurances that keep our mouths open and proclaiming God's good news are stronger still:

- We have the assurance that we are *never* alone.

- We have the assurance that *no one* and *nothing* can harm
  us, even if we're put to death.

- We have the assurance that our labor is never in vain.

- We have the assurance that though we are incompetent,
  nothing is too difficult for the Lord.

- We have the assurance that whether we're rejected by
  people or not, we are beloved and accepted by the Lord.

Paul's victory over his fears in Corinth didn't just set the
course for the remainder of his life; his victory has impacted
world events up to this very moment in time. Let me explain.

Sometime later during one of his stays in Corinth, Paul wrote his letter to the Romans—the letter in which he declared, *"I am not ashamed of the gospel"* (Romans 1:16); the letter in which he declared, *"If God is for us, who is against us?"* (Romans 8:31); and the letter in which he declared that nothing *"will be able to separate us from the love of God that is in Christ Jesus our Lord"* (Romans 8:39).

It was the theological truth that the just shall live by faith, expressed in Romans 1:17, that changed Luther's life. It was a sermon from the book of Romans that captured John Wesley's heart. God has used the book of Romans, written in Corinth, to launch revivals throughout history that are still impacting lives today. We are the spiritual beneficiaries of the victory Paul experienced in Corinth, when, by God's grace, he chose not to be frightened, not to be silent, but to speak.

Moses and Paul came to grips with their bouts of cowardice. It's probably fair to say that all of us are cowards by nature. Because of the fall, all of us fear. But if we have to be cowards, then may God bless us with the cowardice of Moses or Paul.

FOUR

WALKING AWAY FROM GOD

We believers aren't the only ones who wrestle with fears. Just as we have barriers that keep us from proclaiming the good news, nonbelievers have barriers that keep them from receiving it. We need to be aware of those barriers so that we can deal with the genuine objections in people's hearts rather than with the stated objections on their lips.

Let me tell you another story.

On three separate occasions, Konnie came very close to surrendering her heart to the Lord. But each time, as she hovered over the threshold of faith, she backed away instead. One afternoon, I decided to write a letter to Konnie, spelling out the gospel message once more in clear and very personal terms. I followed up a few days later with a telephone call. "Did you get my letter?" I asked.

"I did," Konnie said.

"So, what did you think?"

"What a letter!" she quipped with mock adulation. "You know, Avi, you should have been a writer!"

"I meant the *content*, Konnie. What did you think of *that?*"

I expected another flippant comeback. Instead, she said in a soft, earnest voice, "I think everything you wrote to me is true."

Her answer startled me for a moment. But then I said, "So, pray with me, Konnie. Ask Him to forgive you and make a simple promise to follow Him."

She sighed very deeply. "Avi, how can you be so smart and so stupid at the same time? Don't you understand? I can't."

Konnie couldn't. Why not?

DISBELIEF: A DEFAULT AND A DETERMINED CHOICE

In the Gospel of Matthew, we read about a rich young ruler who asked Jesus, "*What good thing shall I do that I may obtain eternal life?*" (Matthew 19:16). There's great irony embedded in this passage of Scripture. The young man had the right desire. When he inquired of the Lord, he didn't ask for anything sordid or perishable. He asked about obtaining eternal life.

The young man also had the beginning of a correct theological understanding of salvation. Though he mistakenly thought that salvation could be obtained or acquired through the performance of some "*good thing,*" he understood in part that good deeds weren't good enough. For, when Jesus reminded him of the commandments, he replied, *"All these I have kept; what am I still lacking?"* (verse 20). Finally, Yeshua gave him an explicit answer that amounted to putting Him first, above every other consideration: *"Sell your possessions and give to the poor, and **you will have treasure in heaven; and come, follow Me"** (Matthew 19:21). Despite that unequivocal guarantee of eternal life, the young man chose to walk away. How could that be?

> **BECAUSE OF THE FALL, IT'S NATURAL FOR US TO CHOOSE TO DISBELIEVE, TO DISTRUST, AND TO WALK AWAY.**

In a sense, it's really not as incomprehensible as we might think. Because of the fall—when Adam and Eve disobeyed God, fell from perfection, and brought evil into His perfect world—it's natural for us to disbelieve, to distrust, and to walk away. But our disbelief isn't just our spiritual default; it's our determined choice. So often, we're resolved not to believe, no matter what evidence we might be shown.

THE BLEEDING CORPSE

Famed psychologist Abraham Maslow was fond of telling a story about a patient who was convinced that he was dead. No matter what Maslow showed him or told him, the patient insisted that he was a corpse. Then the doctor decided to ask him, "Do corpses bleed?"

"No, of course not," the patient retorted.

After gaining the patient's permission, Maslow pricked the man's finger. And of course, it started to bleed.

The patient experienced an epiphany. "Corpses *do* bleed!" he exclaimed.

So often, even if we know that what we've seen and heard is true, we choose to walk away—like this patient...and like the rich young man who talked with the Lord.

How can that be? We have many reasons. Let me mention just a few.

THE DISGRACE OF THE CHURCH

During our exile in Babylon, God reproached us through the words of the prophet Ezekiel:

> *It is not for your sake, house of Israel, that I am about to act,*
> *but for My holy name, which you have profaned among the*
> *nations where you went.*   (Ezekiel 36:22)

God had chosen us to be a light to the nations. But rather than embrace the call to be a holy people and a kingdom of priests, we practiced the abominations of the nations surrounding us. As a result, we profaned God's name and compromised His testimony to the peoples that He longed to reach.

During the past two thousand years, how often has God's church deserved that same scathing reproach that His holy name has been profaned? How often have nonbelievers rightly castigated the church for her failure to demonstrate the love and compassion that permeated and flowed from every act that Jesus performed and from every word that Jesus spoke? Even worse, how often has the church practiced and condoned—either through active endorsement or passive silence—the most horrific crimes in the name of Christ? The Holocaust stands out as a vivid and shameful case in point.

The tragedy doesn't end there. How many of our own children have turned their backs on the biblical faith because of the lies and hypocrisy of family members, or because of the betrayals and abuses committed by those whom they trusted in the body of Messiah?

What can we say to history's justified indictment of the church? Simply, and modestly, this: We mustn't blame Jesus for the crimes committed in His name any more than we can blame the practice of medicine for the atrocities committed at Auschwitz by Dr. Josef Mengele in the name of medical science. We don't blame medical science; we blame Mengele. And we still go to doctors when we're sick.

What can we say to loved ones who once professed a faith in the Lord, but then walked away because of the lies, betrayals, and abuse that they endured? Simply, modestly, and repentantly this: Jesus never lied. Jesus never abused or betrayed you. Jesus never took advantage of your trust.

> **JESUS NEVER LIED. JESUS NEVER ABUSED OR BETRAYED YOU. JESUS NEVER TOOK ADVANTAGE OF YOUR TRUST.**

We cannot undo the ungodly history of evil men and women who often claimed to act in Yeshua's name. We cannot retract the words and acts that *we've* committed that have caused strangers, friends, and even loved ones to stumble and fall. But we *can* point people to the Lord, and we can urge them to consider *Him*. And where we stand guilty, we can and must repent and resolve to live lives that glorify, not dishonor, His name.

What else can cause people to walk away?

THE SIMPLICITY OF THE GOSPEL

The professor let his secretary know that he didn't want to be disturbed. Then he came back to his desk, invited me to sit down in an adjacent chair, and beckoned with opened palms, as if to say, "Go ahead, I'm listening." And he did listen very attentively, as I explained the core of the message from portions of the Prophets and the Gospel accounts. When I'd finished, he asked, "Is that it?"

I nodded. "That's it," I said.

He lowered his head in thought, and then admitted in a very sad voice, "I can't believe that."

"Why not?" I asked.

He looked up. "Anybody can believe that."

The apostle Paul explained that we Jews want incredible signs while gentiles search for wisdom. (See 1 Corinthians 1:23.)

We don't want a simple gospel that anyone can understand and believe—we want a difficult gospel that we have to struggle to comprehend. Why? Because, if the gospel requires great effort and intellect to fathom it, and if you and I do manage to do so, that makes a remarkable statement about *us*. It highlights how *exceptional* we are.

> WE WANT THE GOSPEL TO BE COMPLEX TO THE POINT OF NEAR INCOMPREHENSIBILITY BECAUSE THAT WOULD HIGHLIGHT HOW EXCEPTIONAL WE ARE IF WE UNDERSTAND IT.

Not only do we want the gospel to be complex to the point of near incomprehensibility, we want the message to be communicated through, and evidenced by, extraordinary, irrefutable signs and wonders. This, too, puts us in a special league. For who can dare challenge the validity of what I declare to be God's incomparable and personalized revelation just to me?

The appeal to our pride underlies the lure of every religious system, every mystical experience, and every path of esoteric knowledge that promises to usher us into the presence of God and make us equal to Him. By contrast, *"we preach Christ crucified,"* Paul says—just the mundane, nonspectacular, easy-to-understand gospel. A stumbling block and nonsense to many, but true, just the same.

We must never apologize for what God, in His infinite grace, chose to make simple enough for all of us to understand. Simple or not, nonspectacular or not, the gospel is true. This is the distinction we must help people see.

What other reasons can cause us to walk away, even if we know that the message is true?

THE ACCOUNTABILITY OF THE GOSPEL

Paul told an unbelieving audience on Mars Hill that God *"has set a day on which He will judge the world in righteousness through a Man whom He has appointed"* (Acts 17:31). I've discovered that for many alleged atheists, the real problem isn't the existence of God, but His authority. They simply will not permit themselves to accept the notion of a sentient being to whom we'll give an account.

Aldous Huxley, the prominent British philosopher and atheist, candidly admitted that he rejected the God of the Bible not just on supposedly intellectual grounds, but because he didn't want any moral constraints or expectations placed upon his life. In his book *Ends and Means,* he wrote:

> I had motives for not wanting the world to have a meaning…For myself, as, no doubt, for most of my contemporaries, the philosophy of meaninglessness was essentially an instrument of liberation…from a certain system of morality. We objected to the morality because it interfered with our sexual freedom.[2]

If we're going to be held to a standard and called into account, then oftentimes, we'd rather decline and walk away, even if we know that the gospel is true.

What else can cause us to walk away, even if we know or at least suspect that the gospel is true?

THE STIGMA OF GOSPEL ASSOCIATION

In the Gospel of Luke, we read about a man who unreservedly told the Lord, *"I will follow You wherever You go"* (Luke 9:57). Which one of us who believes hasn't experienced that same joyous surge of passion for the Lord at some time in our lives? But which one of us wouldn't shrink back, at least a bit, if we heard the Lord tell us what He told the man who expressed such fervent devotion? *"The foxes have holes and the birds of the sky have nests, but the Son of Man has nowhere to lay His head"* (verse 58).

It's quite comfortable to declare unabashedly that we're with Him when society holds Him in high regard. But when

---

2. Aldous Huxley, *Ends and Means: An Enquiry into the Nature of Ideals and into the Methods Employed for Their Realization* (London: Chatto & Windus, 1941), 270, 273.

He's regarded as the One whom the prophet Isaiah described as *"despised and abandoned by men"* (Isaiah 53:3), then the declaration of emphatic allegiance rolls off our lips a little less readily. There's a stigma attached to belonging to the Lord. And if there isn't, then there ought to be. Jesus told us that we must expect to face the hostility of the world because of our association with Him.

> *Remember the word that I said to you: "A servant is not greater than his master." If they persecuted me, they will also persecute you. If they kept my word, they will also keep yours.*   (John 15:20 ESV)

There's more to the matter. The stigma extends from our identification with Jesus to our identification with those whom He's called His own. That can be a serious impediment to non-believers. At times, it can also be a daunting challenge to those who've already believed. Writing from prison near the end of his life, Paul felt the need to exhort Timothy:

> *Do not be ashamed of the testimony of our Lord **or of me** His prisoner, but join with me in suffering for the gospel according to the power of God.*   (2 Timothy 1:8)

We're called to associate unashamedly with the Lord and with others whom we might not ordinarily include in our personal inner circle. Think, for a moment, of the uncanny love and the unnatural mutual allegiance that's suggested by the makeup of the early congregations: Jews, gentiles, male, female, bond servants, and free people. That broke all of the societal rules of the day! Think of the social sacrifice that Lydia, a successful businesswoman, willingly made in order to associate with a

Roman jailor and a slave girl who'd been freed from a demon. (See Acts 16:12–15, 40.)

> **THE GOSPEL CALLS US TO LOVE THE UNLOVELY AND IDENTIFY WITH THOSE WHOM THE WORLD WRITES OFF.**

The gospel calls us to love the unlovely and identify with those whom the world writes off as intellectually deficient and incapable of getting along without a psychological crutch. For many, that identification constitutes an obstacle too formidable to overcome. Rather than deal with the obstacle, people walk away.

THE IRRELEVANCE OF THE GOSPEL

"I don't need Him," Gabor told me. "Jesus is just a crutch."

He didn't always feel that way. Some years before, Gabor had run to the Lord for refuge from a father whose emotional assaults severely threatened Gabor's mental and physical health. Then his father died, and so did the assaults. In time, so did Gabor's perceived need for Jesus. With input from a counsellor, he came to the conclusion that Jesus had merely provided a solution in a time of crisis. But now that the crisis had passed, the need for the solution no longer existed. Gabor concluded that Jesus was irrelevant, so Gabor walked away.

"Don't bother me with that Jesus stuff," he told me over a cup of coffee.

"What if the gospel is true?" I softly challenged.

"Truth," Gabor scoffed. Then he gave me an update on his new passion: jazz.

Pontius Pilate also scoffed. When he asked Yeshua, *"What is truth?"* (John 18:38), it wasn't a real question. It was a dismissive statement, meant to end the conversation, because Pilate had more pressing matters to worry about. A delegation of priests and elders stood nearby, demanding the death of the One they'd recently delivered to him. A sizeable and potentially riotous mob had already gathered in his courtyard. Pilate's own wife had sent him a hasty message, urging him not to embroil himself in the conflict between Yeshua and the leaders of the people. Sending Jesus off to Herod Antipas hadn't helped matters at all because Herod had simply sent Him back.

As a result, when Jesus remarked that He'd come into the world *"to testify to the truth. Everyone who is of the truth listens to My voice"* (John 18:37), Pilate had neither the time nor the desire to enter into a serious discussion. Truth wasn't relevant to all the other circumstances closing in on him at that moment; at least, that's what he must have thought. As a way of ending the interrogation, he scornfully asked, *"What is truth?"* and walked away.

But Pilate *did* know the truth. He knew that the leaders had delivered Yeshua out of jealousy. He knew that the Man standing before him had committed no offense requiring death. He knew that the King of the Jewish people presented no political threat to Roman rule at that time. But the overall challenge to the peace required immediate and expedient action, not a consideration of *truth*.

> **SOMETIMES WE DISMISS JESUS BECAUSE WE DEEM HIM IRRELEVANT TO WHAT'S GOING ON IN OUR LIVES.**

Today, we generally dismiss Jesus for much less dramatic reasons. We don't have any riots to quell. We just don't have the time or inclination to deal with Him right now, even if we know or at least suspect that His claims are true. Perhaps we'll pick up the conversation later on. But for now, we deem Him irrelevant to what's going on in our lives. Like Pilate, we turn away and go out. But *Jesus* doesn't turn away. He's always standing right in front of us, just like He stood before Pilate. He's always ready to engage us with the truth.

THE OFFENSE OF THE GOSPEL

The gospel itself also causes people to feel offended and walk away. What could possibly be offensive about God's message of undeserved love, unmerited mercy, and unearned grace? Just that. Salvation is undeserved, unmerited, and unearned.

If we're determined to try to purchase God's favor by living a scrupulously religious life, the gospel message is nothing less than scandalous. Whether our religion is western or eastern, ancient or novel, Scripture says our own good deeds are as good as *"filthy rags"* (Isaiah 64:6 kjv). Pleasing God doesn't come about through painstaking effort or by traveling the high road of spiritual enlightenment. Rather, it comes about by traveling the low road of humility—specifically, the humility that's required in order to believe that the only Righteous One is Yeshua, who died for us, the unrighteous. Rather than choosing to travel that low road, we take offense and walk away.

> SOME FIND THE GOSPEL OFFENSIVE BECAUSE THEY WANT TO SEE JUSTICE METED OUT WITHOUT MERCY.

There's another type of person who finds the gospel offensive and therefore walks away: those who want to see justice meted out without mercy. Sadly, that often describes those of us who have already believed. The gospel is offensive because it's just too forgiving to too many people. God's pardon is available on the same terms to everyone, even those whom we despise and want to see writhing beneath the wrath of God.

I like the prophet Jonah. I can understand perfectly well his desire to flee from the task of carrying God's word to our archenemies in Nineveh. I can also understand his rage when these enemies repented—thanks to Jonah, no less!—and when God, in His unfathomable compassion and mercy, chose to spare them the judgment that they deserved. (See book of Jonah.)

We need to be uncomfortably frank with ourselves. Which one of us doesn't balk at God's commandment to love and feed our enemies, to bless them when they curse us, and to pray for them when we're abused? Which one of us doesn't bristle at God's declaration, *"I will be gracious to whom I will be gracious, and will show mercy on whom I will show mercy"* (Exodus 33:19 ESV; see also Romans 9:15), when that mercy is showered upon someone we despise?

At the end of the book of Jonah, God challenges the prophet with a disturbing question: *"Should I not also have compassion on Nineveh?"* (Jonah 4:11). The book ends with the question unanswered, as though God were leveling the challenge at each one of us. But rather than deal with it, we choose to walk away.

There's at least one other type of person who can find the gospel so offensive that they turn from it—the person who's been victimized by others. Without a doubt, the gospel brings unmatched consolation to those who've been marginalized and abused. What measureless comfort we find in the arms of a Savior who has suffered all that we have suffered and more. But at the same time, the gospel calls us to confess the sins that *we* have committed, rather than cry out against the injustices that others have committed against us. For those who've been victimized, this can be brutally hard and offensive to the core. An offense that deep can cause many to walk away. But not always.

FINDING YESHUA LATE IN LIFE

Let me tell you about Judit. As a child, she escaped Nazi Germany on a *Kindertransport*, one of the trains that allowed Jewish children to flee the country before the war broke out. Decades later, when she closed her eyes, she could still see the scowling faces and hear the catcalls of gentile peasant children who pelted her boxcar with stones and cries of "Christ killer" as the train passed through the local villages on its journey out.

In England, she survived the Blitz. After the war, she married a nice Jewish man who gave her two sons and then dropped dead, leaving her on her own to fend for her family and herself. She made her way to Canada, where she miraculously found her mother, who had managed to escape the Holocaust after giving Judit over to the *Kindertransport*. But Judit's mother had built a new life for herself that didn't include a reunion with a grown child who had children of her own. Next stop, America, where Judit married a kindhearted widower who could never really love any woman except his deceased first wife.

Despite everything that she'd endured, Judit believed in God, and she clutched fervently to the belief that He would punish the wicked and vindicate the righteous. The only problem is, Judit counted herself as one of the righteous because of all the evil that others had done to her. Her thinking had no room for the notion that she might need to repent of any wrongdoing of her own.

But by God's grace, that changed.

In her late eighties, Judit was diagnosed with Alzheimer's disease. But before her ability to make mental connections began to fade, a remarkable shift in her character took place. She still recalled the abuse and injustices that she'd endured, but the bitterness faded, and gratefulness took its place.

"Something or Someone always protected me," she told me one afternoon. "It's *beshert*." She used a Yiddish word meaning destiny or blind luck.

I politely disagreed. "It's not *beshert*," I told her. "It's the Messiah's mercy and love. He watches over us because He's waiting for us to repent and come to Him."

She leaned close to my face and spoke in a low voice, like a conspirator telling me a dangerous secret. "You know, I pray to Him every night."

I took that as my cue to open my Bible, and I asked her to read some verses from Isaiah:

> *He was pierced for our transgressions; he was crushed for our iniquities; upon him was the chastisement that brought us peace, and with his wounds we are healed. All we like sheep have gone astray; we have turned—every one—to his own way; and the* Lord *has laid on him the iniquity of us all.*   (Isaiah 53:5–6 esv)

After reading the verses, she said, "Every night, I thank Him for keeping me alive."

"Have you ever thanked Him for dying for your sins?"

A look of innocent surprise came to her face, as though she'd stumbled upon an oversight. "No," she said. "I never did."

"Would you like to?" I asked.

She thought for a brief second and then said, "Yes, I would."

There are so many reasons that buttress our disbelief, so many reasons that prompt us to walk away, even when we know or at least suspect that the message may be true. I'll mention just one more.

THE COST OF THE GOSPEL

Salvation is the free gift of God. We cannot earn it. We'll never deserve it. It cannot be bought. But when we believe the gospel message and repent, we do pay a price. For those of us who come from what may be called *gospel-resistant cultures* that have built bulwarks against the penetration of the good news, we pay the price as soon as we publicly believe. In fact, even before we believe, we know that if we merely consider the claims of Yeshua with an open mind and in an open manner, then we're not just breaking ranks with our peers; we're committing cultural treason in their eyes.

Once, I spoke with a rabbi who was one of the *rising stars* in his local Jewish community. He laid out his reasons for why "J" (he wouldn't say His name) might be the "Christ of the nations," but why He couldn't possibly be the Messiah of us Jews. When he'd finished, I said, "Rabbi, those aren't your real reasons."

"Yes, they are," he told me.

"No, they're not. I know your real reason." We stared silently at each other for a moment, locked in an impasse. Then I said, "May I ask you a question? You don't have to answer it." He nodded, cautiously, and I went on. "If you came to the conclusion that Yeshua is the Messiah, according to Moses and the Prophets, and if you openly endorsed that point of view…" I paused, then asked, "What would you lose?"

Quietly, respectfully, I spelled out the cost, as though I were voicing his thoughts out loud for him. "You'd lose your wife. You'd lose your children. You'd lose your livelihood. You'd lose the respect and friendship of everyone who knows you. The consequences would be so severe. Am I right?"

I'll never forget his answer. He said nothing at all. Why not? Because he was a man of integrity. He couldn't admit that I'd spoken the truth. But he couldn't lie and tell me that I was wrong. So, he said nothing.

I'd like to think that a man whose heart is governed by that kind of integrity will someday find the courage to believe, despite the cost. But for now, the rabbi *walked away*, like the rich young ruler who walked away from the Lord.

> **JESUS DIDN'T CHASE AFTER THAT RICH YOUNG RULER, BUT I SUSPECT HE WATCHED WITH DEEP SORROW AS THE YOUNG MAN TURNED AND LEFT.**

Jesus didn't chase after that rich young ruler, but I suspect He watched with deep sorrow as the young man turned and left. I can hear that sorrow in Yeshua's words when He told His disciples, *"It is easier for a camel to go through the eye of a needle, than for a rich person to enter the kingdom of God"* (Matthew 19:24).

The disciples marveled and wondered how anyone could be saved. So Jesus explained, *"With people this is impossible, but with God all things are possible"* (verse 26).

This is our boundless hope. This is the lifeline that we seize and cling to our chests as we weep for our loved ones who have walked away. *"With God all things are possible."*

We have so many reasons for walking away, even when our hearts tell us that the message is true. Given the power of these reasons, those who have already believed might wonder, "Is there any value in helping friends, family, loved ones and even strangers understand the real reasons that hold them back?" Yes, there is. Once the truth is exposed, it becomes harder for many to hide behind the fiction, or to export that fiction to others. The truth *does* set us free, even if the freeing feels like a wrenching away. I'm convinced that it became harder and harder for the rabbi to hide behind his theological justifications, once his real objection—the cost—had been exposed.

In a very real sense, each one of us is just like that rabbi or the rich young ruler before we come to faith. Each one of us possesses riches that we're afraid we'll lose if we choose to believe. But Yeshua, in His grace, makes each one of us poor in spirit so that we might inherit the kingdom of God, regardless of the cost. He makes the riches of heaven so much more valuable than the treasures of earth. As a result, our hearts are able to say with the apostle Paul, *"I count all things to be loss in view of the surpassing value of knowing Christ Jesus my Lord"* (Philippians 3:8).

According to a wonderful tradition in some churches in Central Asia, the rich young ruler who walked away from Jesus was a young Levite of Cyprian birth named Joseph. Most of us know him better as Barnabas, the other name that's given to him in the book of Acts. Barnabas sold a tract of land he owned, gave the proceeds to the disciples for the poor, and followed Jesus wherever He led. It's a lovely tradition, but is it true? We'll have to ask Barnabas after Jesus has come back.

FIVE

COMPELLED TO PROCLAIM

The work in Ukraine and Russia had been going well—unexpectedly and undeservedly well. My wife Ruth and I had followed our probe trip in 1990 with a move to Odessa in 1991. Within a year and a half, the Lord had not only produced an evangelistic harvest, He'd raised up a new generation of Soviet-born harvesters to work in the field. By August 1993, we were set to launch our first full-scale Moscow street-witnessing campaign. My friend Jim Melnick came to Moscow on behalf of the Lausanne Consultation on Jewish Evangelism to encourage us. But he brought with him a very challenging question. He asked if the recent decisions by the Duma, the Russian parliament, would affect any of our plans.

I remember stiffening. "What decisions?" I asked.

"I thought you knew," he said. Then he explained: restrictions of the 1990 Law on Freedom of Conscience and Religion had passed the first "reading." The second reading was pending. After that, the restrictions would become law.

I didn't know what to say. But Jim knew. "Avi," he offered softly, "let's pray."

I don't remember the words of Jim's prayer, but I remember mine. I asked the Lord to forgive me for presuming that the doors He'd opened would remain open without end. I asked Him to forgive me for lacking the diligence to do all that I knew He'd wanted me to do. I begged Him—literally begged Him—to hold back the sun, like He'd held back the sun for Joshua.

He did. He has. Despite waves of governmental attempts to close the doors, God has kept the doors open to this day.

For three decades, my Russian colleagues and I have tried to guard ourselves from presumption. And I've kept my eyes on the sun.

> **MANY OF THE EARLIEST FOLLOWERS OF YESHUA INCESSANTLY PROCLAIMED THEIR FAITH WHEREVER THEY WENT, OFTEN IN THE FACE OF GREAT PERIL AND SEVERE OPPOSITION.**

We know from the biblical record that so many of the earliest followers of Yeshua incessantly proclaimed their faith wherever they went, often in the face of great peril and severe opposition. After the martyrdom of Stephen, a fierce persecution erupted against those first Jewish believers.

While the apostles remained entrenched in Jerusalem, the *ordinary* disciples fled. In their fleeing, you'd think they would have kept silent about their faith in order to avoid calling attention to themselves. But they didn't. Instead, they shared the good news wherever they went, first with their fellow Jews, then with gentiles. They couldn't keep quiet about what they knew to be true.

Years later, the apostle Paul, writing to the believers in Rome whom he hadn't yet met, applauded them because the news of their faith had made waves throughout the empire. They, too, couldn't keep quiet about their faith. The gospel even reached what is now modern-day Iran and Iraq.

How do I know? For a while, my colleagues and I explored the idea of launching an outreach in Tehran, in order to reach the fifteen thousand or so Jewish people living in Iran's capital city. The timing was off, and the outreach still hasn't taken place. But during that season of initial planning, I held a number of strategic meetings with an Iranian believer who worked for a Christian radio program. One afternoon, I asked him, "Aside from us bringing the Scriptures with us into the Babylonian captivity, when did the gospel first get to Iran in the current era?"

He smiled patiently, as if to say, "You should already know this, Avi." Then he opened his Bible to Acts 2 and pointed to the list of places from which Jewish people and gentile proselytes had traveled to Jerusalem to celebrate Shavuot or Pentecost. He read off three names: Parthians, Elamites, and Medes. "Welcome to Iran and Iraq," he said.

What drove these early believers to proclaim their faith so passionately and so persistently? What compelled them to proclaim?

THE REALITY OF THE RESURRECTION

These men and women knew in their hearts as well as in their heads that Jesus had been raised from the dead, and they simply couldn't keep quiet about that marvelous news. After the two disheartened disciples from Emmaus realized who had been walking in their midst, they ran all the way back to Jerusalem that very night, then burst upon the eleven apostles and declared, *"The Lord has really risen!"* (Luke 24:34).

Many other indisputable appearances of the risen Lord occurred after that. Paul reminds the Corinthians that after Yeshua's crucifixion, He appeared not only to Peter, James, and the apostles, but also *"to more than five hundred brothers and sisters at one time"* (1 Corinthians 15:6). But many others had *not* seen Him. Even so, they knew that He'd been raised from the dead. The resurrection was a reality to them, and they had to spread the good news.

> **THE RESURRECTION PROVED THAT JESUS HAD PAID THE PRICE FOR OUR SINS AND WAS NOW SITTING AT THE RIGHT HAND OF THE FATHER, INTERCEDING FOR US.**

Why? Not just because of the miraculous nature of the event, though that very news, in and of itself, demanded a declaration. Believers couldn't be silent because the resurrection made it clear that Jesus had accomplished what He'd promised He would do. This meant that His claims about Himself were true. The resurrection proved that He'd paid the price for our sins. It also proved that He now sat at the right hand of the

Father, interceding for us. And it proved that He would come again to judge the living and the dead.

How could they keep silent about such earth-shaking and imperative news?

What else drove the early believers to proclaim their faith so passionately and so persistently?

THE HOLY SPIRIT COMPELLED THEM TO SPEAK

On that first Shavuot following the resurrection, God's Spirit fell upon the believers. Then He drove them into the temple courtyards, where they proclaimed *"the mighty deeds of God"* (Acts 2:11) in the native languages of the people who'd gathered in Jerusalem for the feast. They *had* to proclaim, even though most of them apparently had no knowledge of the various tongues they were using. But God's Spirit filled them, and silence was an impossibility.

On that same occasion, Peter stood up in the midst of the crowd and delivered a blistering, convicting gospel message to the specific people who had called for the Lord's execution just a few short weeks before. (See Acts 2:14–36.) What compelled Peter to seize that moment to speak? Did he merely recognize a ripe opportunity and grab hold of it? No. This is the same apostle who had succumbed to fear and had denied the Lord three times on the night that Yeshua was arrested and tried. (See John 18:15–27.) This is the same apostle who cowered with the others behind closed doors out of fear for their lives. (See John 20:19.) But now, God's Spirit compelled Peter to proclaim.

It makes perfect sense that God's Spirit should fill and compel the disciples to proclaim the gospel at Pentecost. In biblical times, Pentecost marked the launch of the wheat harvest, according to the Jewish calendar. What a beautiful parallel! For on that first Pentecost some fifty days after the death and resurrection of the Lord, the Holy Spirit launched a gospel harvest that has been going on for nearly two thousand years. But there could be no gospel harvest without the sowing of gospel seed. So, the Spirit compelled them to proclaim.

> **THE GOSPEL PROCLAMATION DURING PENTECOST WAS THE VERY FIRST MANIFESTATION OF THE SPIRIT'S FILLING.**

We shouldn't fail to take note of a fact that might make some of us uncomfortable. The very first time that the Spirit filled the disciples, He filled them for no other reason than to empower them to proclaim. In other words, gospel proclamation was the very first manifestation of the Spirit's filling.

SURRENDERED TO THE LORD'S AUTHORITY

What else compelled the early believers to proclaim? *They were surrendered to His absolute authority.*

One instance where we see this uncompromising surrender to Jesus's authority occurs in the fifth chapter of the book of Acts, following the apostles' second and third arrests. Matters had been heating up—so much so, in fact, that the high priest and the Sadducees felt obligated to act. We're told that the apostles were arrested again and thrown into jail.

But during the night an angel of the Lord opened the gates of the prison, and leading them out, he said, "Go, stand and speak to the people in the temple area the whole message of this Life."   (Acts 5:19–20)

Notice that no promise of protection followed the angel's commandment from the Lord! In light of the Sanhedrin's hostility, combined with the absence of any assurance, the cautious, even *sensible* thing might have been to amend their methodology and lay low for a bit before resuming their evangelistic preaching. But the apostles didn't do that. Instead, *"upon hearing this, they entered into the temple area about daybreak and began to teach"* (verse 21).

Another arrest followed as soon as the authorities discovered that the apostles were proclaiming the gospel once again. The high priest barked, *"We gave you strict orders not to continue teaching in this name"* (verse 28).

But Peter replied, *"We must obey God rather than men"* (verse 29).

Why did the apostles take such an unshakable stand? Certainly, they were emboldened through their prayer, through the signs and wonders that had been taking place through their ministry, and through their earlier miraculous release from prison. But bolstering their resolve was their commitment to be obedient to the Lord, regardless of the consequences or cost.

FILLED WITH LOVE FOR THE LORD

What else compelled these believers to proclaim? *They loved the One who sent them out.*

They loved Him for who He is, and they loved Him for what He'd done for them, just like the prophets before them. Isaiah wrote:

> I will give thanks to You, LORD; for although You were angry with me, Your anger is turned away, and You comfort me. Behold, God is my salvation, I will trust and not be afraid; for the LORD GOD is my strength and song, and He has become my salvation. (Isaiah 12:1–2)

Nearly eight hundred years later, and filled with the same love for God, the apostle Paul all but blurted out:

> I thank Christ Jesus our Lord, who has strengthened me, because He considered me faithful, putting me into service, even though I was previously a blasphemer and a persecutor and a violent aggressor…Now to the King eternal, immortal, invisible, the only God, be honor and glory forever and ever. Amen. (1 Timothy 1:12–13, 17)

When he wrote those words, Paul had already been beaten, imprisoned, flogged, and stoned in the course of his missionary endeavors. He'd faced dangers and had endured persecutions from his own Jewish people, from gentiles, and from false believers. What compelled him to carry on with his work? Love for the Lord.

> **LOVE FOR THE LORD COMPELLED PAUL, PETER, AND THE REST OF YESHUA'S FOLLOWERS TO PROCLAIM THE GOOD NEWS.**

When Paul and his traveling companions spent the night in Caesarea on their way back to Jerusalem, the prophet Agabus foretold all of them what awaited the apostle: he would be bound by Jewish opponents and delivered into the hands of the gentiles. Upon the pronouncement of that word, the others pleaded with Paul not to go on. We don't know how long he listened to their pleas, but we do know how he finally replied. *"I am ready not only to be bound, but even to die in Jerusalem for the name of the Lord Jesus"* (Acts 21:13). This certainly wasn't bravado. This wasn't even zeal. This was love.

Peter, too, carried that love for the Lord in his heart. I sometimes wonder what he thought and felt before the Lord spoke to him at that breakfast on the beach some days after the resurrection. We know that when John pointed out the Lord some distance off, Peter threw himself into the sea in order to get to Jesus on the shore before any of the others. (See John 21:4–7.) We know that, even earlier, Peter and John had raced to the empty tomb. Now, when Jesus asked Peter three times whether he loved Him, the question broke his heart.

> *And he said to Him, "Lord, You know all things; You know that I love You." Jesus said to him, "Tend My sheep."*
>
> (John 21:17)

With those simple words, Yeshua reinstated the apostle who had denied Him three times.

That was all that Peter needed to hear. Future missteps and hesitations notwithstanding, the fisherman's love for the Lord compelled him to spend the rest of his life telling others who Jesus was and what He'd done.

LEARNING TO LOVE THE LOST

What else compelled the early believers to proclaim the good news? *They learned to love the ones whom Jesus loved—the lost and hurting people of the world.*

Once again, we see this most emphatically in the life of Paul. Moments after being pulled away from a mob of Jewish men who had tried to kill him in the temple courtyard, Paul begged the Roman commander to let him speak to that very mob. (See Acts 21:27–40.) Common sense might have moved Paul to let the commander take him out of harm's way. But Paul couldn't do that. A love for the lost compelled him to appeal to the people who had just tried to put him to death.

Unquestionably, the clearest demonstration of Paul's love for the lost can be seen in the words that he dictated in his letter to the congregation at Rome:

> *I have great sorrow and unceasing grief in my heart. For I could wish that I myself were accursed, separated from Christ for the sake of my countrymen, my kinsmen according to the flesh.* (Romans 9:2–3)

Paul wrote these words about some of his fiercest opponents. I suspect he even pictured some of their faces when he dictated those words to Tertius. (See Romans 16:22.) Paul loved these people so much that, if possible, he would have forfeited his own relationship with the Lord if such a sacrifice could have secured their salvation. His love for them made no sense whatsoever, except for one fact: it reflected the Lord's love for the lost.

One day during our Moscow witnessing campaign in the summer of 1996, we came back from the streets and gathered in the flat that we were using as a makeshift base of operations. It had been a difficult time on the streets. We'd experienced unbelief from our own Jewish people, physical hostility from anti-Semites, and interference from the police, even though our activities were legal according to the new Russian laws. (The Lord had held back the sun for three years by that time.) But the results outweighed the hardships and the risks. Everyone came back with a good handful of *contacts*—names and addresses or phone numbers so that we could stay in touch with the people who'd spoken with us on the streets.

> PAUL LOVED THE LOST SO MUCH THAT HE WOULD HAVE FORFEITED HIS OWN RELATIONSHIP WITH THE LORD IF SUCH A SACRIFICE COULD HAVE SECURED THEIR SALVATION.

As the different leaders collected the contact cards from the members of their teams, my eyes drifted over to a young volunteer named Tanya. She sat in a corner, looking very tired and staring with blank eyes straight ahead. In her hand, she held the contact cards of the people she had met. When her team leader reached out to take the information from her, Tanya's hand clenched into a fist around the cards. Then she started to cry, silently, almost with no expression on her face. The tears just traveled slowly down her cheeks. I understood. The cards in her hand were more than pieces of information to her. They were people—lost people. Though she'd only just met them, she loved them with a love from the Lord.

Tanya cried. I'm certain Paul cried as well.

A GRAVE MATTER AND URGENT TIMES

What else compelled the early believers to proclaim their faith so passionately and so persistently? *They understood the gravity of the matter and the urgency of the times.*

Jesus said some very unpleasant and uncomfortable things:

> *I am not of this world. Therefore I said to you that you will die in your sins; for unless you believe that I am, you will die in your sins.*   (John 8:23–24)

> *For every careless word that people speak, they will give an account of it on the day of judgment.*   (Matthew 12:36)

> *Unless you repent, you will all likewise perish.*
>   (Luke 13:3, 5)

Jesus drew an unmistakable distinction between those who repented and believed in Him, and the disobedient who did not. The latter *"will go away into eternal punishment, but the righteous into eternal life"* (Matthew 25:46).

The apostles were just as candid with their words. The first time Peter stood as a defendant before the Sanhedrin, he told the seventy-one religious leaders of our people, *"There is salvation in no one else; for there is no other name* [other than Yeshua's] *under heaven that has been given among mankind by which we must be saved"* (Acts 4:12). In the same fashion, Paul ended his words to his countrymen in the synagogue at Pisidian Antioch with a frightful but fervent plea: *"Beware, therefore, lest what is said in the Prophets should come about: 'Look, you scoffers, be astounded and perish'"* (Acts 13:40–41 ESV).

Why so direct? Because, like their Lord, the apostles understood the gravity of the matter. They understood that whether or not people believed was a matter of life and death. It still is. They understood that the rewards of receiving Jesus are inestimable, and the consequences of rejecting Him are horrific.

They also understood that time is short. An urgency propelled the efforts of believers like Paul. We can hear that urgency when he writes to the believers in Ephesus, exhorting them to make the most of their time, *because the days are evil* (Ephesians 5:16).

Jesus Himself made it abundantly clear. *"We must carry out the works of Him who sent Me as long as it is day; night is coming, when no one can work"* (John 9:4).

Time, as we understand it, is a finite commodity. Even if this current age lasts another five hundred years, time is still short because life is short. Those of us who already believe have a finite amount of time to speak. Those who haven't yet believed have a finite amount of time to hear.

The reality of the resurrection, the infilling of God's Spirit, a commitment to surrender to His absolute authority, a love for the Lord, a love for the lost, and an understanding of the gravity and urgency of the times—these are some of the motives that compelled the early believers to proclaim the good news, regardless of the peril, regardless of the price. At least one more motive needs to be mentioned here...

> WE MUST CARRY OUT THE WORKS THAT JESUS TAUGHT US "BECAUSE THE DAYS ARE EVIL" AND "NIGHT IS COMING, WHEN NO ONE CAN WORK."

A RECKONING LIES AHEAD

The early believers **knew** *that they would give an account.*

God gave Paul a mandate; He called him to be the apostle to the gentiles. To accomplish that call, He entrusted Paul with the message of the gospel. Paul took that trust very personally, even calling the gospel his own. (See 2 Timothy 2:8.) And in his mind, Paul carried a map. He rejoiced that his efforts promoted the spread of the message throughout the Roman Empire, and he longed to bring the gospel to Spain, which was the edge of the known world at that time. (See Romans 15:28.)

We know that despite all of the hardships that he endured, Paul thanked God for the privilege of being called into service. (See 1 Timothy 1:12.) His words also tell us that he knew he would be held accountable for what he'd done.

For we must all appear before the judgment seat of Christ, so that each one may receive compensation for his deeds done through the body, in accordance with what he has done, whether good or bad. (2 Corinthians 5:10)

At the end of his life, Paul could write his own epitaph:

I have fought the good fight, I have finished the course, I have kept the faith; in the future there is reserved for me the crown of righteousness, which the Lord, the righteous Judge, will award to me on that day; and not only to me, but also to all who have loved His appearing. (2 Timothy 4:7–8)

It's an epitaph that all of us should desire.

WHAT ABOUT US? DO WE FEEL COMPELLED?

Can we muster and maintain something of the evangelistic zeal that characterized the lives of our ancestors in the faith? Yes, we certainly can—and for the same reasons.

"The Lord has risen indeed" (Luke 24:34 ESV).

Even though most of us have never seen Yeshua's face or heard His audible voice, we can be gripped with the same certainty of His resurrection that gripped the apostles and compelled them to proclaim. Scripture even commends us to do so.

Though you have not seen Him, you love Him, and though you do not see Him now, but believe in Him, you greatly rejoice with joy inexpressible and full of glory.

(1 Peter 1:8)

Can we experience the same Holy Spirit power of God that compelled the apostles and early disciples to proclaim? Yes. But we need to face an unpleasant truth about ourselves. Ironically, there are times when we do indeed sense that same Spirit-led compulsion, but then we choose to dismiss His urging because we dislike what He's calling us to do—to speak. And so, rather than yield to the Spirit's compelling power, we resist and walk away from the doors that God has opened up.

Desiring His power in our lives must be grounded in a readiness and commitment to be used however He chooses to use us, including the unashamed proclamation of His good news.

Can we surrender absolutely to His absolute authority? Can we commit to a surrender that compels us to proclaim? We must. In some ways, however, this might be our greatest challenge. Our hearts are braced from birth to revolt against His authority, and we wage that rebellion throughout our entire lives—even, sad to say, as believers. But when God rescues us, He replaces our hearts of stone with hearts of flesh, and He places His own Spirit within us. That new heart of flesh enables us to know the will and ways of the Lord. And His Spirit empowers us to walk in his statutes and obey His commandment to proclaim. (See Ezekiel 36:25–27.)

> **DESIRING THE HOLY SPIRIT'S POWER IN OUR LIVES MUST BE GROUNDED IN A READINESS AND COMMITMENT TO BE USED HOWEVER HE CHOOSES TO USE US.**

Can we be filled with a love for the Lord that compels us to proclaim? Yes, certainly we can. As the patriarchs, prophets, and apostles loved Him for who He is, so we love Him for who He is. *"Jesus Christ is the same yesterday and today, and forever"* (Hebrews 13:8). As believers in biblical times loved Him for what He'd done in their lives, so we love Him today for what He's done for us. During the moments when our love turns cool, all we have to do is ask Him to remind us of just a portion of the many times He's answered our prayers and intervened in our lives.

Can His love for the lost become our own? Yes. God demonstrated His love for us by sending His Son to rescue us from perishing. Now, that same love from the Father, shed abroad in our hearts, compels us to proclaim what God has done.

Do we understand what the early believers understood—that without the Lord, people enter eternity cut off from God? I pray that we do. The gospel is not just good news; the gospel is urgent news. Embracing that truth will compel us to proclaim.

I write these words at age sixty-nine, and I've had the privilege of speaking to my people about our Messiah for more than forty years. It's been a good four decades. It's been a fast four decades. Do I have another forty years to preach the gospel? Not likely.

Do I have another ten years? Do I have another five? I hope I may have many years left. But I'm not presuming. I'm keeping my eyes on the sun.

God knows my days. For my part, I only know that night is coming, which means that either He returns, or I die and go to be with Him. Neither scenario is a tragedy. But once I'm with Him, I won't be preaching the gospel. This is the only time that I have.

This is the only time that you and I have.

He will hold us accountable for what we did with the gospel that He placed into our hands. When we stand before Him and give an account, how good it will be when we hear Him say, "Well done."

CONCLUSION:
MY FAVORITE LEPERS

When you think of lepers in the Bible, which ones come to mind? Perhaps you think of the man who knew that Jesus possessed all power and authority in heaven and earth, and therefore pleaded with Him to make him well. (See Matthew 8:1–3.) Or perhaps you remember Naaman, the mighty Syrian general, who needed to humble his heart and dip seven times in the Jordan in order to be cleansed. (See 2 Kings 5:1–14.)

I often think of the four lepers we encounter in 2 Kings 7:3–10. Samaria, the capital city of the northern kingdom of Israel, is under siege by the Arameans, and the people behind the city walls are facing certain death by starvation. When we first meet the four lepers, they're sitting outside the city gates, which is where we'd expect lepers to be sitting in that society. The threat of contagion made them outcasts from everyone except their own.

There's something wonderfully sublime, even tender, in the way they assess their own dilemma. They reason that if they stay outside the city gates, they'll eventually die, but if they enter the city, nothing but death awaits them there as well. One other course of action remains, but it's such an out-of-the-box option that only their resignation to the reality of their plight could have brought it to their minds.

They say to one another, "*Now then come, and let's go over to the camp of the Arameans. If they spare us, we will live; and if they kill us, then we will die*" (verse 4). In other words, "What do we have to lose?"

So, they go. And to their utter astonishment, they stumble upon more than mere survival; they encounter abundant life.

The Arameans have abandoned their tents, leaving everything behind—animals, equipment, clothing, gold, silver, and food. The night before, the Lord had caused these invaders to hear the clamor of advancing armies. In a panic, they'd deserted their camp and had fled for their lives.

No one has to tell the lepers what to do next. First, they devour the food. Then, they travel from tent to tent, ransacking the goods and hiding the valuables in a safe and secret place. Then it hits them. They realize:

> *We are not doing the right thing. This day is a day of good news, but we are keeping silent about it; if we wait until the morning light, punishment will overtake us. Now then*

come, let's go and inform the king's household.

(2 Kings 7:9)

I can't help wondering whether any of the lepers recoiled at the thought of going back to tell the others the good news. Did one of them, perhaps, say or at least think, "Who's going to listen to us? We're lepers. We have no credibility. Better to stay where we are and just thank God for the rescue that He's given to *us*."

THEY COULD NOT KEEP SILENT

Whether that part of the conversation ever took place or not, that's not what happens next. Staying put and keeping silent about the salvation they've found simply isn't an option. How can they be silent? They know that silence is wrong. They know that silence will prove fatal to the others in the city. And they know that silence puts them in danger of some sort of punishment or accountability. So, they travel back to the city gate and announce the good news to the gatekeeper on the walls.

Amazingly, the gatekeeper doesn't kill them or even berate them for delivering such outlandish news. Neither does he shoo them away. Most likely, his own hunger has made him desperate for any promise of relief. He passes the report along—all the way up to the royal household.

The king's response isn't too surprising. He thinks it's a ploy by the Arameans to lure him into a trap. But one of the king's retinue pleads, *"Have some men take five of the horses that remain…let us send them and see"* (verse 13). By God's grace, the king consents.

They discover that what the lepers have reported is true.

The day ends as a day of salvation. The people are rescued from death.

All because the lepers resolved to go and tell.

POSTSCRIPT:
THANK YOU FOR READING

If you're not yet a believer in Yeshua, I want to thank you for reading this book anyway. If you know in your heart that the message is true, but you've never taken the step of repenting of your sins and asking Jesus to pardon you, I invite you to take that step right now. To make it easier, let me offer you a model prayer that you can read. If you direct the words to the Lord, He'll hear you, and He'll respond:

> Lord Jesus, I know that my life doesn't please You. I'm living in rebellion against You, but I want to turn around. I believe that You died for my sins and rose from the dead. Please forgive me. Please give me the strength to turn away from all I do and believe that displeases

You. From this moment on, I will openly follow You. In Jesus's name, I pray. Amen.

If you prayed that prayer, asking Him to forgive you and asking Him to change you, then I can tell you that He did forgive you, He has changed you, and He will continue to work in your life, making you more like Him every day.

To memorialize this moment, this step of faith that you have just taken, I suggest that you sign your name and date below:

_____

Name   Date

If you're not quite ready to utter that prayer, I invite you to contact me at avi.snyder@jewsforjesus.org. You and I have already started a conversation with each other through this book. So, let's talk some more.

ABOUT THE AUTHOR

Avi Snyder grew up in a traditional Jewish home in New York and New Jersey. In his early twenties, he defined himself as a Jewish atheist. But in 1975, a tract from Jews for Jesus challenged him to consider Yeshua's messianic claims. Thanks to that tract and the faithful witness of Christian friends, Avi gave his heart to the Lord in March 1977. He graduated from Fuller Theological Seminary's School of World Missions with a master's degree in missiology.

Avi married Ruth in late 1977, and in 1978, they joined the staff of Jews for Jesus. Throughout the 1980s, Avi led the work in Los Angeles. During that time, he won a landmark case in the United States Supreme Court against Los Angeles International Airport. The airport had sought to prohibit his right to distribute free religious literature on the terminal's grounds, which was designated as public property.

In the late 1980s, Ruth and Avi caught a vision for reaching the Jewish people in the unravelling USSR. A probe team excursion in 1990 led to them moving to Odessa, Ukraine, a year later. Today, indigenous Jews for Jesus teams share the good news in cities in Russia, Ukraine, and Belarus.

Avi and Ruth came out of Russia in 1998 in order to oversee leadership transitions, first in New York and then in London. But all the while, Avi's sights were fixed on Germany because of the growing influx of Jewish people who were emigrating from the collapsed USSR. Today, a team of Jews for Jesus now brings the gospel to the Jewish population of Berlin. In addition to German-born Jews and Jewish people from the former USSR, some twenty thousand Israeli expatriates now call Berlin their home.

Outside of the former USSR, the largest indigenous Jewish population in Central and Eastern Europe resides in Hungary—nearly one hundred thousand people, most of them living in Budapest. In 2011, Avi and Ruth moved to Budapest to establish another Jews for Jesus outreach. Ten years later, Hungarian-born Jews for Jesus conduct a thriving ministry, especially among Jewish intellectuals and Holocaust survivors.

Avi's heart has always rested in Central and Eastern Europe. He says, "We Jewish believers in Yeshua have a moral obligation to return to the lands where we died, proclaiming God's message of life to Jews and non-Jews alike." That conviction has given birth to a new project called *Life from the Dead*. In August 2021, Avi coordinated an international, inter-ministry team of twenty-five workers during a two-week outreach in Warsaw, Poland. The composition of the team itself bore witness to the truthfulness of the gospel message, with Jews, Poles, Germans, and people from the former Soviet Union standing shoulder to shoulder, testifying of the love of the Lord. "What a redemption of history," Avi says. "What a testimony of the reconciling power of His cross."

Avi is the author of a number of articles and tracts, as well as the book *Jews Don't Need Jesus—and Other Misconceptions*. He and Ruth currently live in the States, where Avi serves as the Jews for Jesus European ambassador. They have three grown children: Leah, Joel, and Elizabeth.

For more information about Jews for Jesus,
visit jewsforjesus.org.